Lives in Cricket: No

Bill Copson

More Than Miner Interest

Kit Bartlett

With a foreword by Eric Midwinter

First published in Great Britain by
Association of Cricket Statisticians and Historians
Cardiff CF11 9XR
© ACS, 2008

British Library Cataloguing-in-Publication Data.
A catalogue record for this book is available from the British
Library.

ISBN: 978 1 905138 60 9
Typeset by Limlow Books

Contents

Foreword

By Eric Midwinter

Not only coal, but also culture, was the product of the British mining communities, especially in the first half of the twentieth century. For the highbrows, there was D.H.Lawrence's highly-charged novel, *Sons and Lovers* (1913). For the middlebrows, there was A.J.Cronin's *The Stars Look Down* (1935). For the lowbrows, there were the 'flicks', with a small genre of colliery films. We became well acquainted with the poignant gloom of the pit disaster and watched as Michael Redgrave sought, anachronistically but aptly, to be upwardly mobile, desiring a life above ground.

Sporting lore was a feature of the cult. There was apparently a ready availability of footballers and cricketers, chiefly quick bowlers, such as Harold Larwood, in the pits. It was supposed that football league club directors or county cricket club committee members would whistle down the mineshaft and up would pop such a hero. Like so many Ronnie Ronaldes, these administrative *siffleurs* were part of the legend.

Bill Copson, working down Morton Colliery from the age of fourteen, was characteristic of this breed, although it was, seemingly, during the enforced leisure of the abortive General Strike in 1926 that his gleaming talent was spotted. Ten years later he was drilling his way through many a county batting order, as the bradawl of the locally hewn Derbyshire team that, with resolution and solidity, won the 1936 County Championship. Kit Bartlett's welcome and telling biography describes the life of this stalwart who shifted himself effortlessly from, so to say, one seam to another.

Why do we find these tales of doughty county servants so satisfying? Certainly they sentimentally remind us of a lost world, with units of cricketing itinerants criss-crossing the nation on wheezing steam trains, and playing over thirty first-class games a summer, and there is little harm in such brazen nostalgia. Nor should we forget that, over against the pleasant aspects, these were decades of gross economic injustice and harsh social censoriousness. But perhaps it goes a little deeper than that. There is a profound attraction in the wholesome attitudes and simple values of the likes of Bill Copson and his fellow-professionals. Indeed, in what has been called the 'pathological individualism' of modern existence, and for all the benefits of its material comforts, we would soon be searching for the hidden agenda and the psychological axe-grinding of anyone in public life who exhibited such wholesome traits. We have come frighteningly close to suspecting sincerity and to spotting hypocrisy round every selfish corner.

For all their individual foibles and idiosyncrasies — several of them, inevitably, displeasing — the English cricket professionals of the mid-twentieth century presented a collegiate ethic of some force and worth. There is much to learn as well as enjoy in this, just as there is in the similar collective ethic of several groups of craftsmen and tradesmen, miners included, of that day.

Bill Copson was a superb fast bowler and a laudable representative of a craft that was remarkable for both its skills and its credo.

Sunday best.
Bill Copson almost 'modelling' his England blazer, 1939.

Chapter One
Early Days and Family Origins

The year 2008 sees the centenary of the birth of one of Derbyshire's most respected and devastating quick bowlers. William Henry Copson, generally known of course as Bill, was an extremely dangerous, auburn-haired pace bowler who, in his relatively short first-class career of some twelve English seasons, accomplished a number of remarkable bowling performances for Derbyshire. In particular, he played a most important part in helping Derbyshire to win, in 1936, their only County Championship title to date. The county has had a long tradition of producing effective fast bowlers and Bill Copson can certainly take his place in their forefront.

He can be considered somewhat unlucky to have only played in three Test Matches, two of which were at the time when he had reached the peak of his career in 1939. He was one of so many cricketers whose career was so abruptly cut off by the outbreak of the Second World War. To lose six full seasons at the age of thirty one, when he had just reached Test Match status, must have been a major blow to him. He did achieve selection for MCC's 1936/37 tour to Australia and New Zealand as a result of his splendid season in 1936, but was unable to break into the Test side ahead of such experienced bowlers as Bill Voce, Gubby Allen and Kenneth Farnes.

William Henry Copson was born at 324 High Street, Stonebroom, a small village near Chesterfield in North-East Derbyshire on 27 April, 1908: the house where he was born no longer stands. For many years his date of birth was erroneously recorded as 1909 in reference books. It was often the practice in those days for cricketers joining a professional county staff to understate their age, sometimes by two or more years, in order that they might be able to stay longer in the game as retirement approached. If he had deliberately misinformed the county, perhaps he was simply following the example of his county colleague, Harry Elliott, who on first joining the Derbyshire playing staff gave his date of birth as 2 November, 1895 when his correct date was 2 November, 1891. Elliott was thus twenty eight when he made his first-class debut in 1920, not twenty four, and played his last games for the county in 1947 aged nearly fifty six when recalled in an emergency.[1] It is possible of course that this may have been entirely unintentional on Bill's part, as production of a birth certificate would not necessarily have been obligatory when seeking employment in those days. When asked his age at some time before joining the Derbyshire staff in 1932 he may have given the impression that he was approaching twenty three instead of twenty four, and this became fixed for a while in record books.

It was not until 1979, eight years after his death, that Bill Copson's birth date was correctly recorded in the Derbyshire Yearbook as a result of research by the late Frank Peach, the much respected Yearbook editor and county's statistician for many years, who had undertaken the huge task of verifying and correcting births and deaths for all the county's first-class cricketers. Other reference books quickly followed suit. It is still somewhat surprising however, that the birth details of Copson, a Test cricketer, were apparently never checked at any time during his first-class career.

The name Copson is a variant of Cobson, meaning son of Jacob, and this name can be traced back to the thirteenth century. Many Copsons can be found in the Northamptonshire and Leicestershire areas of the country. There is also a village in Leicestershire called Copston Magna which may have a connection with the derivation of the family name. Stephen Copson, a bricklayer, was born in 1808 and had a son called William Henry Copson, grandfather of the cricketer, who was born in 1844 in Thornby, Leicestershire. He was also a bricklayer and married Emma Hurst on 19 November, 1869 and had a son also called William Henry, born in Gumley, Leicestershire in 1872, who worked first for the Midland Railway Company initially at Belper as a railway porter. He subsequently moved to Stretton, not far from Chesterfield, where he boarded with the Stevens family in a railway cottage attached to the station: here he met his future wife, Hannah, a daughter of the family. This station, which was on the Midland line from Nottingham to Chesterfield, has since closed. Bill's father subsequently took

---

[1]   In an article in *The Cricket Statistician* in 2000, the late Philip Thorn listed some twenty four English cricketers who had 'shifted' their birth dates forward by four years or more. Pride of place, if that is the correct phrase, went to William Wilkinson, who played five matches for Nottinghamshire in 1892 and 1893, and who brought his birth date forward by ten years.

employment as a coalminer at Morton Colliery a few miles from Stretton.

Bill was the second eldest son of the seven children of William Henry senior and Hannah Stevens who had married in 1900. His other siblings were Minnie, born and died in 1901, Constance Mary (1902-1973), Robert Alfred (1904-1913), Gwennie May (1906-1943), Horace (1910-1926), and Clarence (1916-1984). Robert, three years older than Bill, was killed very tragically in a gunpowder accident on 1 February, 1913. The details of this unfortunate event are worth recording. He and a few young friends had been helping his father to clear out the cellar of the general grocer's shop, whose proprietor was a Mr John Rayworth, which adjoined their home in the High Street. An unused 'bobbin' of gunpowder, which was frequently used in mines to dislodge hard-forming seams of coal, had been left in a tin canister and had probably lain there untouched and forgotten about for some fifteen years. A number of candles were being used by the group as there was no other form of illumination. The boys thought that the canister resembled a toffee tin and went to examine it more closely by holding the candle close to the bobbin. There was a huge explosion and Robert was very severely burned. The father, William Henry senior, was also badly injured, but recovered later in hospital. Robert was rushed to hospital but unfortunately did not recover and died early the following morning. In a small mining settlement like Stonebroom, with a strong sense of the danger of explosives, the tragedy would have affected the whole community. At the subsequent inquest, reported in great detail in the local Press, the Coroner recorded a verdict of accidental death. Bill, who was only four years old at the time, was not in the cellar with the other boys, but no doubt he would have retained a vivid childhood memory of the loss of his older brother.

Stonebroom[2] lies in an area of the Derbyshire and Nottinghamshire coalfield with a strong cricket tradition. Many of the industrial villages and small towns are the birthplaces of

---

2   The name derives from proximity to a local stone quarry and from a once locally prolific yellow-flowering shrub, rather than from any sweeping implement.

cricketers of some renown.[3] The colliery ground at Blackwell, where John Chapman and Arnold Warren created their world record ninth-wicket partnership of 283 for Derbyshire against Warwickshire, in 1910, two years after Copson's birth, is only a couple of miles from Stonebroom. The famous cricket 'nursery' of Sutton-in-Ashfield, just over the Nottinghamshire boundary, is scarcely more than a bus ride away. Coal was once 'king' throughout this area: it had been discovered in the locality by George Stephenson, the railway engineer, when excavating a railway tunnel through Clay Cross Hill in 1837. Morton Colliery, about a mile from Stonebroom, was opened by the Clay Cross Company in 1865 and by 1896 was employing nearly six hundred underground workers at its two mine shafts. The pit at Morton closed in 1964 and today the coal industry in Derbyshire is almost defunct: the last deep mine in the county, at Creswell, closed in 1994 and at the present time, 2008, there are a mere eleven deep-level coal mines in the whole of the United Kingdom, three of which are in the neighbouring county of Nottinghamshire. Stonebroom itself was thus a creation of the nineteenth century coal boom: the 1841 Census identifies two small hamlets, Upper and Lower Stone, with a total of only six dwellings, but by 1895 it had become a considerable village. There was a Methodist chapel in the village from 1875; its Anglican church, St Peter's, was consecrated in 1900, and a local school was built at about the same time. Bill attended this local village school and later, at the age of fourteen, in 1922, started work at the local colliery, this being almost the sole source of employment in the immediate area.

In 1913, shortly after the tragic death of their son Robert, the family decided to move away from Stonebroom and went to live in New Street, Morton, but they returned to Stonebroom after a short period, to a terraced house owned by the Clay Cross Company which employed Bill's father. This house was one of a number specially built in 1900 for the mineworkers which consisted of eight rows, each of twenty dwellings and became known locally as

---

3   More than forty cricketers who have played first-class matches for Derbyshire have been born in the county within a five mile radius of Stonebroom. The only other first-class cricketer born in the village itself was Joseph Humphries, tail end batsman and wicket-keeper, who played 276 first-class matches for the county between 1899 and 1914, and like Copson, three times for England in Tests. He was due to play in his own benefit match for Derbyshire against Nottinghamshire at Chesterfield in June 1920, but the game was abandoned without a ball bowled, the only match in the season where the county avoided defeat. He was on the first-class umpires' list in 1933, standing in 24 matches in all.

*Stonebroom Primary School,
much altered since Bill Copson's time.*

'The Blocks'. They were cramped, badly built, damp, poorly equipped and some families were overcrowded: at one time *The Derbyshire Times* described the conditions in them as 'The Black Hole of Derbyshire'. Although they were less than forty years old, these buildings were eventually condemned by the local council as 'unfit for human habitation' in 1939 but, because of war-time and post war housing shortages, their residents were not rehoused and the buildings demolished until 1950.[4] It is astonishing that these were conditions where a man was brought up who had sufficient strength and stamina to deliver perhaps eight hundred overs of first-class fast bowling a year, and was able to develop himself to a standard sufficient to represent his country as an international sportsman.

Stonebroom was where Bill spent his formative years, as a member of a household where money would have been in extremely short supply. The Welfare State as we know it today was still many years away in the future. Bill's mother, Hannah, died in 1923 so that his father was left to cope, more or less on his own, with a family of five children, although some of the older members of whom were already out at work and therefore presumably made some sort of practical and financial contribution to running the household. No

---

4   It is remarkable to think how poor general housing conditions were in many homes even in the early nineteen fifties, well within living memory of many people today. The author can well recall staying in 1952 at the home of a relative, which had no running water or electricity. Lighting was by oil lamps and water obtained by hand pump. Although this was in rural Dorset, such primitive conditions would not have differed that much from many other parts of Great Britain at that time.

doubt relatives and friends helped Bill Copson senior, in their various ways, to bring up his family.

High Street, Stonebroom,
no longer a pit village, on a quiet afternoon in 2008.

It was often said that Bill looked somewhat undernourished during the early days of his cricket career. Sam Cadman, the Derbyshire coach when Bill started his association with the club, once remarked, 'Trouble is, he's had more dinner times than dinners.' The work of a miner, hewing coal by hand, was an extremely arduous job requiring great stamina and reserves of energy. Although he was not a particularly big man physically, he developed powerful muscles in his arms which stood him in excellent stead when bowling. Cadman, who could turn a phrase, once likened him to a gorilla, because of his long arms and big hands. Donald Carr and Tony Brown have both remarked that he 'seemed to have longer arms than anyone else.' His slightly spare frame would no doubt have been an advantage when working in the extremely confined and cramped areas underground.

Bill Copson, together with his county colleague Tommy Mitchell, are probably the only first-class cricketers and certainly the only Test cricketers who owe the beginnings of their cricket careers entirely to the 1926 General Strike, which took place in May of that year. The Trades Union Congress had called out on indefinite strike all workers in key industries such as the railways, the docks, steel and general transport to support the Miners' Federation, who were striking against wage cuts and longer hours proposed by the mine owners. This strike threat had been postponed from 1925 to allow the Samuel Commission to report on the dispute. At one time over a million and a half such workers were on strike.

Although the General Strike was 'settled' after nine days on 12 May, the miners remained on strike almost until the end of 1926. During the summer months, Copson, now eighteen, often went along with his colleagues to the local recreation ground to play some knockabout games of cricket. He had had no coaching in the niceties of bowling style, but simply ran up to the wicket and bowled right arm as fast as he was able in his own natural way. Many were impressed with his ability to hit the stumps so often. At one stage, he played for a team of striking miners against a Police XI, and this initially brought him to the notice of Morton Colliery Cricket Club, where he soon appeared in the second team. In 1927 he played in the first eleven and played for that side regularly thereafter for some four seasons.[5]

Morton Colliery CC, probably in 1926,
with Bill Copson standing third from the right,
and his father wearing an umpire's coat.

Perhaps we should say something about Bill's employers at this point. Copson and his fellow miners were on strike against the Clay Cross Company which operated the coal mines at Morton where he was employed. The Copson household was also a

---

5   Basil Easterbrook, writing about Copson in the *Wisden* of 1979, suggests that the manner of his rise to cricket excellence was 'so improbable' that if a novelist presented it as a storyline, his credibility would vanish in a flash.

company tenant. The business was founded by George Stephenson in 1837, producing coal, coke and gas, iron and bricks all from sources in and around the town of that name. It was by far the dominant force in the local economy for much of its existence. All the interests in the business were purchased by Sir William Jackson in 1871, as sole proprietor: it became a limited company in 1913 when all its shareholders and directors were members of the Jackson family. Even in 1937, six of the seven directors were Jacksons. The family was closely involved with local sports of various kinds, including the Clay Cross Park and Derbyshire County Cricket Clubs. At the time of the 1926 strike, Guy Rolf Jackson was the Derbyshire captain, a position he held until the end of the 1930 season: he continued to play occasional matches for the county until 1936, sometimes alongside Copson. Guy's older brother Geoffrey, killed in action in the Great War, played briefly for the county and a cousin, Anthony Mather-Jackson, played in the twenties. Paradoxically, Copson joining the strike against the Clay Cross Company in 1926 thus eventually brought a benefit to the Jackson family's other major interest in the Derbyshire County Cricket Club, especially in 1936. When Guy was joint managing director in 1946, the coal mining part of the company was nationalized and it diversified into the aggregates business. Guy Jackson died in 1966 and Copson was a pallbearer at his funeral at Morton Parish Church[6]. The company became part of the Ready Mixed Concrete group in 1974: it ceased to trade in 1998.

Morton Colliery played in the Derbyshire Minor League and Copson performed a number of excellent bowling feats for them. These achievements included seven for 11 against Old Tupton in 1931. Bill then joined the Clay Cross Park Club who played in the Derbyshire League and on one memorable occasion took all ten wickets for five runs against Staveley on 15 August, 1931. He was presented with the ball with which he accomplished this feat at the Annual General Meeting of the club in the following April by Brigadier-General G.M.Jackson, the club's president. This ball was mounted on an ebony plinth and the details of his feat inscribed on a silver shield attached thereto. It was one of Bill's proudest possessions. It is worth giving details of this remarkable

---

6   Michael Copson, Bill's son, recalls that the Jackson family were regularly mentioned at home when he was a child, although of course he did not often understand the significance of the references.

performance. In forty one balls he clean bowled seven batsmen and actually took five wickets for one run in his last eleven balls.

Bill's future Derbyshire colleague, Tommy Armstrong, a slow left arm bowler who had first appeared for the county in 1929, also played for Clay Cross Park at this time. Copson's steady improvement was duly noted by the Morton Colliery secretary, Fred Marsh, who recommended him to the Derbyshire county authorities and he was given a trial at the nets. He also played three games for the Derbyshire Second Eleven this summer but without any conspicuous success.

Chapter Two
Starting in First-Class Cricket

Copson became a professional cricketer when he joined the county staff in April, 1932, just before his twenty fourth birthday. He had not been recruited by the traditional method of whistling down a mineshaft, but the method was close enough to ensure that traditionalists could recognise that 'custom and practice' was being continued.

Derbyshire were at this time an improving team under their new captain, Arthur Richardson, who had become leader in 1931, when he succeeded Guy Jackson. Competition was keen for a place in the first team with Stanley Worthington, Leslie Townsend and Alfred Pope all potential regular opening bowlers. The end of the 1931 season had also seen the retirement, at the age of 41, of Archie Slater, who took 108 wickets that year, to take up a contract with Colne in the Lancashire League, leaving a space for a newcomer. In a rain-reduced second team match at Edgbaston at Whitsun, 1932, Copson took five wickets for 38, including four for 30 in Warwickshire's first innings. Apparently unable to find a replacement for Slater's medium pace, the county gave Bill a chance in the first team in Derbyshire's ninth game of the summer which happened to be against Surrey at Kennington Oval on 8 June. He could not have chosen a better place, apart perhaps from Lord's, to make his first-class debut: events at well known grounds often seem, even to this day, perhaps somewhat unfairly, to attract more attention from the Press, which was certainly the case in this instance.

Copson's feat of taking the wicket of Andrew Sandham with his first ball in first-class cricket is often remembered whenever his name is mentioned. Stanley Worthington had bowled the opening over and, with only four runs on the board, all scored by Jack Hobbs, Bill with his first ball had Sandham well taken at second slip by Charlie Elliott for a duck. Although the Surrey batsman was in his early forties and coming towards the end of his distinguished career, he was still a formidable batsman.[7] Copson also had the valuable experience of bowling against Jack Hobbs, the Master himself, eight years older than Sandham and some two years away from his last first-class season of 1934.

Bill went on to take three further wickets in the innings, bowling T.F.Shepherd and P.G.H.Fender and trapping Douglas Jardine leg before wicket. He finished with the highly respectable debut figures of four for 43, against the formidable Surrey batting line up. *The Times* awarded him a simple headline the following morning, 'Young Bowler's Good Start', referring to his bowling as 'just over medium pace' and to his ability to 'swing the ball a little bit each way.' Under grey skies and with a strong wind blowing, he can scarcely have expected more helpful conditions. The newspapers did not mention that this was Copson's first visit to London and that he was not able to afford a proper pair of cricket boots for the occasion. He played in ill-fitting shoes which, by the time he had reached his twenty fifth and final over, had made his feet start running with blood. It is said that his fellow players cut pieces off his shoes with a razor blade to allow him to continue bowling.

Surrey, however, went on to win the match very comfortably by 199 runs. Copson took a further two wickets in the Surrey second innings, T.F.Shepherd for the second time in the match, and E.W.J.Brooks, the wicket-keeper. Copson was only the second player, after H.G.Curgenven in 1896, to take a wicket for Derbyshire with his first ball on first-class debut for the county. The feat has been accomplished twice subsequently, by F.C.Brailsford and J.G.Wright.

He had further immediate success for Derbyshire in his next two matches, taking five for 48 in the first innings against Hampshire at Southampton and five for 40 at Tonbridge versus Kent. Thus in his first three matches for his county he had taken 17 wickets for 284 runs: shortly after he was awarded his county cap. Copson had a very deceptive pace off the wicket, from quite a short run for a fast bowler. (Frank Thorogood of the *News Chronicle* described it 'as a quiet run-up of six or seven paces', although Eric Hollies once

---

7   Many years later, by one of those strange chances in life, Bill's son Michael was introduced at a new neighbours' house welcoming party when he and his wife moved to Gloucestershire. On exchanging names the host said casually, 'No relation to the cricketer, I suppose?' When Michael replied in the affirmative, he said, 'What a coincidence: my name is George Sandham, nephew of the cricketer.' The two families have been close friends ever since.

remarked wryly to M.J.K.Smith that his own wrist-spinner's run-up, of eleven paces, was about the same length as Copson's.) He had a slight pause before delivery with a high arm and very frequently surprised batsmen who were left playing much too late at the ball. Later in his career the delivery which came into the right-hand batsman was described as 'a genuine off break rather than an inswinger.' Pelham Warner thought he put 'life and venom into every ball.' He could be genuinely hostile and at various times in his career, R.E.S.Wyatt, Patsy Hendren and others were injured when trying to deal with his shorter delivery. Billy Griffith reported that his bowling 'can be very unpleasant indeed.' Batsmen who faced him later in his first-class career found that he bowled 'very straight.'

New kid on the block.
Bill Copson in his first season in first-class cricket.

After this initial flurry of wickets, he regularly opened the bowling with Stan Worthington, but did not take more than three in a single innings until the end of the season.[8] *Wisden* commented favourably in its seasonal notes, stating that he had 'a good action' and 'should do well in the future.' The *News Chronicle Cricket Annual*, less generously, thought him simply 'useful.' He finished the season with 46 Championship wickets at an average of 26.76 from seventeen matches.

Derbyshire had fallen three places in the Championship table this season, finishing in tenth position. Two of their early games were abandoned without a ball being bowled. They went on to record five successive defeats between 1 and 17 June. Altogether, they won only six of their twenty eight matches. Harry Storer headed the batting averages: other batsmen to pass the thousand runs in the season were Stanley Worthington, Leslie Townsend, Denis

---

8   In his sixth match for Derbyshire he played against George Gunn, the eminent Nottinghamshire and England batsman, by then 53 years of age, who had made his first-class debut as far back as 1902. In his last full first-class season in 1949 Copson played in two matches versus Yorkshire who included the eighteen-year-old Brian Close, who did not make his final first-class appearance until 1986. Bill's two opponents between them therefore had a career span of eighty four years.

Smith and the captain Arthur Richardson. Townsend completed the cricketer's double in championship matches alone, the first Derbyshire cricketer to accomplish this feat.

Copson batted for most of the season at No.11: indeed for most of his first-class career he was an unquestioned tailender. He did however manage one batting curiosity in his sixteenth match. This occurred at Taunton when he contributed fifteen runs to a tenth-wicket partnership of 47 with Harry Elliott, the Derbyshire wicket-keeper, in the county's second innings. This survived for almost 72 years, rather freakishly perhaps, as the county's highest tenth-wicket partnership against Somerset until May, 2004, when Mohammad Sheikh and Nick Walker scored 104 in a drawn match at Derby. Off the field, Bill returned to work for the Clay Cross Company, though not now, it would appear, underground as a miner.

* * * * *

In 1933 Bill Copson's bowling advanced rapidly. The Press now reported his bowling as fast-medium, and his captain, with a range of quick bowlers under his control, seems to have taken to using him in short spells. He consolidated his position as a regular opening bowler, playing in twenty six of Derbyshire's twenty eight match Championship programme and took ninety wickets at an average of 21.34.

He started his second season fairly quietly and took five wickets in an innings only once in his first sixteen games. Things looked up a little after this rather lean spell and he finished the season more strongly. He had nine wickets in the return game with Sussex at Hove in late July and then had his first haul of seven wickets in an innings, seven for 62 off 28 overs, in the match against Gloucestershire at Cheltenham College ground in mid-August, where Derbyshire went down to an innings defeat.

Wisden commented favourably on his performance this year saying that 'nothing was more gratifying than the advance of Copson in his second season with the county', adding that his 'pace off the pitch provided an effective contrast to that of the slower bowlers.' *The Cricketer*, in its summary of Derbyshire's season, said he 'makes pace off the ground' and 'in another year or two may well be in the front rank.' Derbyshire finished sixth in the

Championship, winning eleven of their twenty eight matches. Their most successful bowlers, apart from Copson, were L.F.Townsend with 87 wickets, T.B.Mitchell with 136 and T.S.Worthington 50.

Although he did not generally excel as a batsman, he made what proved to be his highest score in first-class cricket, scoring 43 in Derbyshire's last game of the season, against Lancashire at Blackpool. On a soft pitch after his side had reached 135 for nine, he helped to add 80 runs for the last wicket with his captain, A.W.Richardson. In scoring a six and seven fours, *Wisden* thought he revealed 'unknown skill'. He was a right-handed batsman and usually went in at either number ten or eleven in the order: he reached 25 runs in a first-class innings only six times in all, and throughout his career his average never rose to double figures. Nevertheless he did on a number of occasions during his career help to add valuable runs in late wicket partnerships: the largest of these are given in the Appendix. He seems rarely to have been selected as a night watchman; but every now and then he joined the defiant 'big hitter' school of fast bowlers with a couple of sixes, sometimes cross-batted off the back foot.

* * * * *

By now Copson was beginning to be noticed outside Derbyshire as an extremely promising fast bowler and the 1934 season certainly added to his growing reputation as a dangerous performer whose faster ball frequently led to opposing batsmen being deceived as to his pace. He took ninety-one first-class wickets at an improved average of 18.10 runs. He managed to take five wickets in an innings on only three occasions however. He did, though, miss seven games through injury, after straining a leg in the third match of the season, at Derby. Statistically his best return was five for 36 at Tunbridge Wells against Kent at the beginning of July.

He played his first ever game against an Australian team when the tourists visited Chesterfield. This attracted a large crowd which no doubt would have included a number of his immediate family, friends and colleagues. Copson failed to take a wicket in this match. He did however have the daunting experience of bowling against Don Bradman and Bill Woodfull in this his second full season in the game.

Derbyshire improved their final standing in the County Championship by rising to third position, behind Lancashire and Sussex, the county's highest position since returning to the competition in 1895. They won twelve of their twenty eight games. Eight of these were won in the second half of the season. They won three out of their last four games and completed a fine double over their close rivals, Nottinghamshire. Tommy Mitchell, the leg spinner, had a splendid season with 138 wickets and was selected for two Test Matches. *Wisden*, in its seasonal comments on the county's performance, said that Derbyshire 'had few if any superiors as a bowling combination.' Referring to Copson, the Almanack said that 'many competent judges predicted a brilliant future for him', and that 'many of the best batsmen found his late swerve and pace off the pitch difficult to counter.' The *News Chronicle Cricket Annual* also reported that 'good judges think he is a future England bowler.'

* * * * *

Copson's fourth season in first-class cricket, in 1935, saw his progress falter. Because of injury he missed matches in early June,

Bill Copson training with Chesterfield FC at Saltergate in January, 1936. Seventy years on, are fast bowlers still expected to head heavy footballs?

at the start of July and then at the end of August, appearing in only eighteen of Derbyshire's twenty eight Championship fixtures, taking seventy one wickets. At the end of June the county sent him to Skegness, the Lincolnshire seaside resort, well known for its bracing airs, to regain his health. Examinations by specialists in the summer and in January revealed that he was suffering from a strained sacroiliac joint at the lower extremity of his back, a not uncommon sports injury. As part of the remedy he was sent in the following January to train with Chesterfield Football Club, then a member of the Football League's Third Division North. The training

21

regime there gave him a far more robust physique, adding about a stone to his weight, and set him up for the following summer's splendid achievements. He had a much better second half of the season, with a nine wicket aggregate in the match against Gloucestershire at Burton-on-Trent, and six Sussex wickets in an innings at Hove in early August.

Derbyshire finished the season in second place to Yorkshire, having at one period, at the end of June, headed the table. A defeat by that county at Scarborough in mid-August finally put paid to any chance of their becoming champions. They won as many as sixteen matches, a record number, out of twenty eight, many by comfortable margins. They started the season in convincing fashion, winning four consecutive games in May, each of them in two days, and had a splendid victory over Somerset at Derby when they dismissed that county in the second innings for only 35 runs. Copson played a very important part in this victory taking five wickets for fifteen runs in their opponents' rout.[9] Although his appearances for the county were intermittent, Copson had nevertheless established himself as a match-winning bowler. Derbyshire had won twelve of the eighteen Championship matches in which he played: the county played ten games when he was absent; of these they won only four.

The two Pope brothers, George and Alfred, had excellent seasons for their county, with much improved records in both batting and bowling. Mitchell had another splendid season taking as many as 160 Championship wickets, a new record for the county. This included all ten in an innings against Leicestershire at Leicester for sixty four runs. Denis Smith had an outstanding season with the bat scoring 1,697 Championship runs at an average of 42.42. He made his Test debut against the visiting South Africans in the Third Test Match at Headingley, making 36 and 57. He was also selected for the unofficial winter's tour to Australasia in the side captained by E.R.T.Holmes of Surrey which played fourteen first-class matches.

After the season had ended, the uncertainty Bill must have felt about his cricket career was no doubt softened when on Thursday, 21 November, 1935, he was married at the Church of the Holy

---

9   In his autobiography, Bill Andrews refers to the pace of Copson's bowling in the second innings of this match. Somerset were set 150 to win in ninety minutes. Opening the batting, Andrews was yorked middle stump first ball, with his bat 'still in the air.' Somerset's collapse followed.

Cross at Morton, the parish church, by the Rector, Rev W.L.Latham. His bride was Emily Titterton, the youngest daughter of Mr and Mrs Charles Titterton of The Broadleys, Clay Cross. She worked for the Globe Tea Company in its general provisions store in Clay Cross – expertise which enabled her later to run her own shop: she helped run the local Girls' Friendly Society and was involved with amateur dramatics. The occasion was full of cricket connections.[10] Bill was 'supported' by his youngest brother Clarence, who played League cricket in the Derbyshire League. The bride's father was Charles Titterton, the scorer for the Clay Cross Park Club which was where Emily and Bill met. On their marriage, the couple moved to a house in Hepthorne Lane, North Wingfield, a village about five miles north of Stonebroom.

Bill and Emily Copson at the seaside, 1935

10   The *News Chronicle Annual* reported of Copson in the early thirties that 'the vicar of his parish had brought him to the notice of the Peak county.'

Chapter Three
Annus Mirabilis

Looking back, British and European news in the year 1936 seems to be characterised by events which we now think of as unusual, if not unique. The abdication of King Edward VIII to enable him to marry Mrs Wallis Simpson, a twice divorced American; the huge hunger march by the unemployed from Jarrow to Westminster; the re-occupation of the Rhineland by German troops; and the invasion of what was then called Abyssinia by the Italian army, were all unconnected events which fitted that pattern.

In its own less momentous way, Derbyshire's achievement in winning the County Championship, for the first and only time, follows that trend.[11] The success was not only unique, but it was unusual in that it was only the second time that a county outside the 'Big Six' had taken the title.[12] For Copson this rather wet summer was one of conspicuous success. His accurate and very hostile fast bowling played a key role in his team's triumph. His

---

11   From 1911 to 1962, *Wisden* recorded Derbyshire as having won the County Championship in 1874, at a time when the title was decided by the Press and not by the clubs themselves. In that season, the county had played four first-class matches, winning three and drawing one. The Almanack had taken into account a book published in 1895 by Alfred Gibson who had decided that 'least matches lost' was the means by which the title champion was awarded. R.S.Holmes published a book in 1896 making a similar identification, and this found its way into *Wisden* regularly from 1911. Later research, including that by members of the Association of Cricket Statisticians and Historians, has shown that contemporary publications judged Gloucestershire to be the best county side, and that the 'least matches lost' method was not in widespread use in 1874. The Derbyshire club did not celebrate its winning of the championship in that year, nor did local newspapers state that the club were champions. An 'official' championship under which the county clubs decided how to allocate the title did not come into operation until 1890. Nowadays *Wisden* says that the 'title of champion county is unreliable' before 1890, but says that its listing including Gloucestershire as the 1874 champion county is 'the most accurate available', but adds that 'it has no official status'.

12   Although it produced sides with a genuine local identity, the requirement which operated until 1939, that players should either be born or live for two years in the county they played for, adversely affected counties with small populations. In the mid-thirties, Derbyshire's resident population was smaller than all but four of the counties in the Championship. The county club's membership was correspondingly small. In 1936, Derbyshire had 2,220 members compared with 3,450 at Kent, 4,649 at Lancashire, 5,465 at Surrey and 6,592 at Yorkshire. This in its turn limited the resources available to develop and maintain teams. Derbyshire's title was thus a very particular achievement.

season was complete when he received the high accolade of selection for the forthcoming winter's tour to Australia and New Zealand.

Derbyshire's triumph was the pinnacle of what had been a steep progression from the depths of their experience in 1920 when, out of eighteen matches played, they had the abysmal record of losing seventeen with the other one abandoned without a ball bowled. They finished bottom again in 1924, but then showed considerable improvement by taking fifth place in 1927. In 1932 they were tenth and then had a very neat arithmetical progression, sixth in 1933, third in 1934 and second in 1935. This led 'naturally' on to their being acclaimed as well deserved and very worthy champions in 1936. They won thirteen out of twenty eight matches, being defeated only four times.

The team's undoubted strength was in their bowling. The county took its championship opponents' wickets, 442 at an average of 18.47,[13] more cheaply than any of its competitors. The principal wicket-takers were Copson with 140 wickets at 12.80; A.V.Pope, Copson's new-ball partner, 94 at 17.72; and Mitchell 116 at 20.45. Between them these three bowled almost three-quarters of Derbyshire's overs. Backing them up, Leslie Townsend had 54 wickets at 19.66 and also scored over 1,000 runs again. Denis Smith, Worthington and Alderman also reached this latter target, although their batting did on occasions let the side down. The side suffered through an injury to George Pope, who had taken 62 wickets at 19.62 in 1935, but who developed cartilage trouble at Bristol in late May and played only four matches in 1936. At the end of the season, Mitchell fractured a thumb whilst batting and missed the last two matches, although by then the title was all but won.

Analysis of Copson's performances throughout this memorable season shows a very consistent record of sustained hostile bowling.[14] Derbyshire began their season by drawing against Hampshire at Southampton and losing decisively to Kent at Gravesend. This match was over before lunch on the second day.

13   In the ten seasons 1930 to 1939, only Yorkshire improved upon this bowling average, with 16.81 in 1931, 17.63 in 1932, 18.23 in 1935 and 18.33 in 1939, all years when they headed the final table.

14   His captain later supported this assessment. Reminiscing on the season some thirty years later, Arthur Richardson said that Copson and Tommy Mitchell were 'at the heart of the Championship victory.' He called them both 'killers . . . positive bowlers . . . and both likely to run through a side.'

Derbyshire had been asked to play an exhibition match, but declined as they wanted to travel home early. Arthur Richardson, the appointed captain, then joined the side and they slipped into gear with three consecutive victories over Surrey, Sussex and Gloucestershire. By this stage of the season, Copson from his first six matches, including a 'friendly' versus Oxford University, had taken thirty three first-class wickets. He had four returns of five or more wickets in an innings during this period. His best performance in these games was undoubtedly in the match versus Surrey at Derby when he took twelve wickets altogether, with returns of five for 33 and seven for 19, his best first-class match and innings performance to date. The visitors were dismissed in their second innings for 77 and *Wisden* referred to Copson's bowling as 'irresistible'. He had a spell of six wickets for eight runs after the tea interval. He took five for 42 in the Sussex first innings in the next match. Further accurate bowling at Northampton followed, when he took six for 24 in 22 overs in the home team's second innings.

His excellent bowling at this stage of the season helped to win him a place in the Test Trial, North *v* South, which took place at Lord's in mid-June. This was his first-ever representative match and the first time that he had played for a first-class team other than Derbyshire. As a trial for the Test matches, the game was alas ruined by bad weather and play only took place on the last two days. Copson only captured one wicket in the match, that of E.R.T.Holmes, but scored 24 runs helping Joseph Hardstaff to add 39 runs for North's tenth wicket. He also held two catches. Although he had bowled extremely well in the season to date, he was unable to gain a place in any of the three Test matches against the visiting All India team. The opening bowlers' places in these games were filled by G.O.B.Allen, A.R.Gover, R.E.S.Wyatt and W.Voce. The rain which affected the Test Trial also brought a draw to Derbyshire's match with Yorkshire at Chesterfield being played at the same time, when the visitors had followed on.

He returned to the Derbyshire side for their next two games against Somerset and Warwickshire, but took only two wickets in the three innings in which he bowled. He was at the top of his form, however, in the next match at Chesterfield against Worcestershire, taking five wickets in their first innings for only 34 runs. The home team won this game by the narrow margin of three wickets. He had identical figures of four for 35 in both innings of the next game, at

Buxton versus Lancashire, where Derbyshire were dismissed for their lowest score of the season, 61, in a rain-interrupted drawn match. The county then won two consecutive matches conclusively by an innings margin against Worcestershire and Warwickshire. In the first of these, at New Road, Bill had most impressive figures of five for 38 and seven for 16, the latter of these being his best innings return to date. At one stage in their first innings Worcestershire had lost half their wickets for six runs. On a rain damaged pitch the county lost their last fourteen wickets for only seventy two runs after lunch on the last day, of which nine were claimed by Copson. They were dismissed for 64 and 47. The victory over Warwickshire placed Derbyshire at the head of the Championship table on 7 July, from which position they were never displaced. Their next game against Hampshire, also at Chesterfield, was the first time that Derbyshire had ever held a cricket week, with two consecutive home matches, at any of their home venues. This match was spoiled by rain, Copson bowling only eleven overs in the game from which he took three wickets. He did not bat or bowl in Derbyshire's next fixture at Old Trafford, where play took place only on the last day.[15]

In the meantime Bill had been selected to appear for Players versus Gentlemen at Lord's. At that time this was the most important fixture in the season's calendar outside the Test matches and was virtually another Test Trial. A player performing well in this showpiece match could enhance his prospects considerably. The Players side was a strong one captained by W.R.Hammond and included several contestants for places in the forthcoming tour of Australia and New Zealand. Rain on the first day washed out play. The match was noteworthy for inspired fast bowling for the Gentlemen by J.W.A.Stephenson and Kenneth Farnes. The former took nine wickets for a mere forty six runs, including three wickets in four balls at one stage in the innings. The Gentlemen, captained by G.O.B.Allen, won the toss and were dismissed for 130 runs. Copson, who shared the opening bowling with Gover, had four wickets for 29 and Gover six for 41. Both bowlers made many deliveries keep unexpectedly low. The Players had a first innings lead of 64 runs and a second innings declaration by The Gentlemen set them 131 to win in 75 minutes. Farnes, with some spectacular bowling, three times sent the stumps of Gimblett,

---

15   This match, incidentally, was the last first-class match in which Derbyshire fielded an entire eleven born within the county.

Hammond and Hardstaff catapulting to the feet of the wicket-keeper Howard Levett and virtually sealed his selection for the tour. The Players finished the match on 63 runs for the loss of five wickets. Bill Copson could feel satisfied with his form in this match and that his name would have been very much still in the selectors' minds.

He maintained his skills in the next Derbyshire match, against the Indian touring team at Derby. The visitors had been heavily defeated in the First Test, at Lord's, and had been going through rather a torrid time, having won only three of their first-class matches at this stage of the season, with two of these being against Ireland and the Minor Counties. Their game against Derbyshire, on 18, 20 and 21 July, was left drawn through an over-cautious declaration by the Indian captain, C.K.Nayudu. Copson took five of the Indian wickets in the first innings for 44 runs. When he dismissed V.M.Merchant in the second innings this was his one hundredth wicket of the season, the first time he had reached this milestone.[16] The bowling averages published in the Press a few days later put him second behind Hedley Verity, who was just short of 150 wickets.

Derbyshire next travelled to Bramall Lane, Sheffield for an important Championship encounter with Yorkshire, at this stage fifth in the table. In a very keenly fought match they missed taking the first innings lead by just two runs, but unfortunately the whole of the second day's play was lost to rain. Bill took six of his opponents' wickets for sixty runs including the much valued ones of Len Hutton and Herbert Sutcliffe, the latter being bowled for a duck. A defeat at Ilkeston by six wickets by Nottinghamshire, close behind in the table where their batting let them down, was their first since mid-June: this brought the neighbours within striking distance in the table. Copson only took one wicket in this match. They won their next encounter, versus Essex at Chelmsford, by the narrow margin of twenty runs. Their opponents had been set 102 runs to win, but succumbed to an inspired spell of bowling by Tommy Mitchell, who took six of the last seven wickets to fall for only twenty five runs.

---

16   Copson himself had little use for these milestones. Will Taylor, the Derbyshire secretary once told him, possibly in this year, that he was approaching a hundred wickets for the season. He replied that he wasn't bothered how many wickets he took 'as long as the side is doing well.'

The scene was now being set for Derbyshire's final run in to their eventual triumph, although there were still some final tremors to be overcome. Their next match was against Surrey at Kennington Oval. The team had gained a first innings lead of 117 runs, with Copson and Mitchell having accounted for nine of Surrey's first innings' wickets. Derbyshire's reply was dominated by a superb innings of 102 from Denis Smith, his first century of the season. A series of dropped catches cost Derbyshire dearly as Surrey totalled 315 for the loss of seven wickets in their second innings, but bad light and rain caused the game to be abandoned as a draw. Copson had a further three wickets to give him a match analysis of seven for 101. They defeated Leicestershire comfortably enough, by nine wickets, in their penultimate home game and Bill distinguished himself by taking three wickets in four balls, making 'the ball leave the turf at bewildering pace' according to the *Wisden* report. He had match figures of nine for 79.

A drawn match at Worksop followed when a last day undefeated opening partnership by W.W.Keeton and C.B.Harris, in three hours and twenty minutes, enabled the home team to draw the game. Copson had a further four wickets in the Nottinghamshire first innings. Derbyshire's last home fixture of the season was against Northamptonshire at Chesterfield and they were very nearly defeated. In the visitors' second innings, a magnificent 241 not out by A.H.Bakewell, in an innings total of 411 for six declared, set the county 347 runs to win but, having lost half their wickets for 64, had to settle for a draw finishing the game on 173 for the loss of seven wickets. Mitchell, when batting in the second innings, was struck on the thumb and could not play again in the season. On their way home from this match Northamptonshire suffered a tragedy when R.P.Northway was killed and Bakewell severely injured in a car accident. The latter's right arm was badly damaged and this innings proved to be his last in the first-class game. Copson had a further four wickets in the Northamptonshire first innings. Although Derbyshire lost their next game at Wells by the narrow margin of one wicket, their second defeat by Somerset during the season, they were duly acclaimed as champions on the early evening of Friday, 28 August, when it became known that Yorkshire only managed a draw in their penultimate match at Hove against Sussex. Copson had a good return in Somerset's second innings with six wickets. Arthur Wellard, the renowned Somerset hitter made 86, striking five consecutive sixes on a ground with short boundaries off Tommy Armstrong, who had been brought in to replace Mitchell and was playing his first county match for over twelve months.

It was an unsatisfactory way to win the title, losing away to Somerset in a small country town, with calculations being made about average points per match, no doubt on the backs of cigarette packets, and with the opposition's big hitter getting his name in the papers. The Press were both kind to Copson and critical of him, as is their wont. *The Times* for example reported of Derbyshire, 'They owe much to Copson, who can come remarkably fast off the pitch and who has again and again taken those quick wickets which are of such immense moral and material importance to a side.' But it added, 'His action is not everything that could be desired, but the wickets fall, and Copson is prominent in the analyses.'

Home grown.
Derbyshire's successful side of 1936.
Standing (l to r): H.Elliott (wk), L.F.Townsend, W.H.Copson, H.Parker (scorer), A.V.Pope, D.Smith, C.S.Elliott.
Seated: H.Storer, T.S.Worthington, A.W.Richardson (captain), T.B.Mitchell, A.E.Alderman.
Readers may perhaps recall that another version of this photograph has the team's masseur, J.Bennett, peering over Copson's shoulder.

The newly acclaimed champions celebrated on their cross-country journey back to the Midlands by train – no doubt more discreetly than they would do now – and travelled to Oakham School, for another 'small town' match, to finish their wonderful season, with an emphatic innings defeat of Leicestershire. The home side were dismissed twice for 151 and 121, Copson finishing his Championship season with a further seven wickets. Derbyshire, having lost Worthington to the first ball of the innings, then had a partnership of 209 by Denis Smith and Stanley Worthington for the second wicket.

Derbyshire's final record in 28 Championship matches was won 13, drawn eleven and lost four. Formal celebrations followed in the county after their return to the county town on 1 September. The team was entertained at The Drill Hall, Derby on that date by the tenth Duke of Devonshire who was Lord Lieutenant of the county and also President of the County Cricket Club. He had left a shooting party at Bolton Abbey in Yorkshire specially. Also present were the Mayors of Glossop, Ilkeston, Chesterfield, Buxton and Burton-on-Trent. A telegram of congratulation was received from Lord Hawke, the President of Yorkshire. The Duke of Devonshire specifically called upon Bill Copson and Stanley Worthington, who had just been selected to tour Australia, to come to the platform to shake hands with him. A dance followed, music being provided by the Fifth Battalion of The Sherwood Foresters, part of the Territorial Army. A testimonial fund was set up for the players, from which later they were all provided with a watch. Above all though, there was pride that the winning of the championship had been achieved by a side comprised largely of players born and coached within the county.[17]

As a result of his outstanding performances during the season Copson gained the honour of selection by the Editor of *Wisden* as one of the Five Cricketers of the Year for 1936 in the following year's edition published early in 1937. The others selections were his playing colleague Stanley Worthington, V.M.Merchant from the Indian tourists, A.R.Gover and C.J.Barnett.

---

17   Derbyshire had fielded twenty players in the season's Championship matches; fifteen were born within the county. The five born outside the county's boundaries made a total of 26 appearances between them. Most of the professionals had been 'brought on' through the County Club's own 'nursery' run by Sam Cadman, who had himself played 375 matches for the county between 1900 and 1926, and who had been the county's coach since 1926.

The entry for Copson gave a fair resumé of his career to date and described how he came into the first-class game. It mentioned that 'his deadly bowling was one of the main factors in Derbyshire winning the Championship' and added that 'Though he had never figured in a Test Match, no surprise was caused when his name appeared in the list of players chosen to participate in the tour to Australia.' Copson finished his wonderful season with a match at the Scarborough Festival, his first at that venue, where the MCC Australian Team took on H.D.G.Leveson Gower's XI. The game was drawn and Bill managed to take only one wicket in each innings, although they were the valuable ones of Sutcliffe and Hendren. In modern terms, his 'image' was now of some commercial worth and it duly appeared in the Churchman's cigarette card series this year, along with those of his county colleagues Denis Smith and Stan Worthington. This trio also appeared in the 1938 Players' series.[18] It is unlikely that he received more than a few pounds from the tobacco companies.

---

18   Like many sportsmen of the time, Copson smoked, though not heavily.

Chapter Four

Australia and New Zealand

All was now set for what was to be, for Bill Copson, the almost unbelievable magic of selection for the MCC team chosen to tour Australia to try to recover The Ashes, which had been surrendered in 1934. Just over four years previously he had been hewing coal underground and had hardly, if ever, ventured away from his native Derbyshire. Away from his usual winter employment with the Clay Cross Company, he was travelling abroad for the first time in his life, meeting people from all walks of life and visiting places about which he could only have read and never dreamed that he would see. The tour was an extremely long one and involved Bill, a newly married man, being away from home for over seven months in the days when the only means of contact with loved ones at home was by the written word or in an emergency by telegraph with its curt language. This is, of course, a tremendous contrast to today's continuous electronic communication, where touring cricketers can be whisked home by air when domestic crises occur or to be present at the births of their children. Kenneth Farnes' mother died during the early part of the tour, but there

Bill Copson's 1936 passport photo: it made no difference to the outcome of the Ashes series.

would have been no question of his being allowed to return home even had he so wanted. Certainly as late as 1954 this view still prevailed when Colin Cowdrey's father died while the MCC were on their way by ship to Australia.

In those days teams were selected in stages for overseas tours. The first seven names to be announced were Allen, Robins, Hammond, Leyland, Verity, Fishlock and Hardstaff. Captain Rupert Howard, the Lancashire secretary, who had played eight matches for his county in the nineteen twenties, was invited to be manager. Nine further names were released on 29 July and 9 August, including that of Copson. When Copson's name was issued at the end of July, the Press suggested that Alf Gover of Surrey 'should have been given preference': this claim is at least debatable. At this stage of the season, Derbyshire were well clear at the head of the championship table and Copson had taken 107 wickets at 12.34, by comparison with Gover's 133 at 17.26. The announcements left one wicket-keeper's place outstanding: this awaited a fitness test on Ames which later proved to be satisfactory. The side was captained by G.O.B.Allen and consisted of seventeen players. Four were amateurs, Allen, Robins, Wyatt and Farnes. Four players, Hammond, Leyland, Duckworth and Ames were making their third visit down under; Allen, Wyatt, Voce and Verity their second; the remaining nine, Copson, Sims, Fishlock, Hardstaff, Robins, Worthington, Farnes, Fagg and Barnett were making their first trip. Worthington and Copson were the only Derbyshire players. Copson was the only member of the side without previous Test experience, and one of only three players who had not played in the three-match series against India in the summer of 1936. In terms of prestige, he thus had the most to do to catch up with the other players. Besides this, he was almost an unknown quantity to his captain and had played against him only twice in first-class cricket before his selection was announced.

It was probably the strongest side that could have been picked. At the last minute Wyatt had replaced E.R.T.Holmes, who had withdrawn for personal and business reasons. Of those who missed being chosen, Gover who had taken two hundred wickets in 1936 and Paynter, a hero of the previous Ashes tour of 1932/33, may have been considered unlucky not to have gone. Gimblett, Stephenson and Bowes must also have been in the selectors' minds and come very close to being chosen. Nevertheless, even with Bowes and Gover left at home, this was a side well-stocked with quicker bowlers: Copson, Farnes and Voce, were specialists, and Allen, Hammond, Worthington and Wyatt were all-rounders with a recognised ability. Competition for the fast bowling places was bound to be strong.

The thirteen professionals all received the sum of £400 for the tour, plus thirty shillings (£1.50) a week spending money on board and £2 on shore. All travelling expenses (excluding drinks), and tips were also given. A bonus was also due to each man at the end of the tour but this varied according to the individual form shown. MCC records show that, of the thirteen professionals, Hammond received the highest bonus of £350 and that Copson, one of four players not to play in a Test Match received £260. The captain received a bonus of £100, the other three amateurs £50, with a request that this should be spent on souvenirs. Amateurs also received an additional allowance of £25 for providing their own equipment.

After a pre-tour dinner at Lord's on 11 September, the side left Waterloo on the boat train for Southampton on 12 September to embark on the Orient Line's *R.M.S.Orion*. The Orient Line was a most successful steamship company that specialised in luxurious ocean travel to many parts of the world. Sister ships in the fleet were the *Orcades* and the *Orontes*. The *Orion* had been built in Barrow-in-Furness and launched in 1935. Her maiden voyage to Australia had only been made in the previous year on 28 September 1935, when she sailed from Tilbury. She carried a crew of 466 and accommodated 708 Cabin class and 700 Tourist class passengers. The ship which was the first British ocean liner to be fitted with air conditioning in all her public rooms, was perhaps the most luxurious on the Australian run at the time, and a huge contrast with the privations of Bill's early life in Stonebroom.

Shipmates.
Stan Worthington and Bill Copson playing quoits on R.M.S.Orion on the way out to Australia.

On the journey to Australia calls were made at Gibraltar, Toulon, Naples, Port Said, Suez, Aden and Colombo, which was reached on 3 October. Bill made shore excursions at all these places as the ship stayed in port for up to a whole day at the various stops. The team played their first match on foreign soil against All Ceylon when they had a comfortable win in what had become a traditional 'pipe opener' for many Australia-bound MCC teams. All Ceylon made 149 for 4 wickets declared and Copson, though 'suffering badly from sea legs' had an economical spell of twelve overs without taking a wicket. The MCC innings of 232 for the loss of five wickets was dominated by an unbroken partnership of 140 between Hardstaff and Allen which was a record for any wicket in these series of matches.

After being ashore for only twelve hours in Colombo, the team re-embarked and their ship set sail for Australia where they arrived at Fremantle in Western Australia at 6am on 13 October. The journey had taken thirty one days which in these days of fast air travel seems like an eternity. Travel within Australia was to be mainly by long distance train: some internal air travel between the various State capitals had by then been established, but MCC declined to sanction this largely for safety reasons. Railway trips were made more tiresome as different State railway gauges often necessitated change of trains at the borders. The longest trip of all was from Perth to South Australia, which included the crossing of the Nullarbor Desert, with its famous three hundred mile length of straight track.

Nevertheless these long sea voyages and railway journeys had a distinct advantage in that cricket teams certainly got to know each other extremely well. Copson would no doubt have shared a cabin with his county colleague Stan Worthington, but would not have known many of the other team members particularly well at the outset of the tour. The tourists tried to keep themselves fit by many forms of deck sports, which also helped to establish a closer team spirit.

The team stayed at the Palace Hotel, Perth for nearly two weeks whilst they played the opening two first-class matches of the tour. MCC had a very comfortable win over Western Australia, not at that time a Sheffield Shield competitor, by an innings and 180 runs. Copson did not play in this game, but was selected for the second match against a Combined XI. The locals had been strengthened by the inclusion of the Australian Test players Fingleton, McCabe and Grimmett, together with a future one, C.L.Badcock. In his first ever first-class match abroad, Copson performed very well. With an undefeated ten runs, he helped his captain to add seventy for the tenth wicket out of an MCC total of

497. He opened the tourists' bowling with Voce and captured four of the home side's wickets for 82 runs. The Combined XI, thanks largely to a record second-wicket partnership of 306 in 235 minutes between Badcock and Horrocks, managed a comfortable draw. MCC ran into difficulties with their wicket-keepers in this game, as both Duckworth(broken finger) and Ames (strained back) were unable to play, so Fagg kept wicket. In the subsequent two matches Tom Wade, the Essex wicket-keeper who was visiting Australia on holiday, was co-opted into the side.

The touring side moved on to the eastern side of Australia by train. They left Perth in the evening of 24 October and took three nights and two whole days before reaching South Australia in the early morning of 27 October. Here they stayed at Bentley's Hotel at Clare for a one day game against a South Australian Country XI, which they won by nine wickets. Copson played in this match but, after taking two wickets for 13, slipped on wet turf during his fifth over, straining his groin.

He then missed the next two first-class matches, against South Australia and Victoria. This was unfortunate for him as he desperately needed match practice if he was to have any chance of making the Test side. He returned to the team for the important game against New South Wales starting on 13 November, when MCC suffered their first defeat of the tour. He could, however, only manage to take three wickets in the match which the home team won easily by 135 runs. Shortly after this match, on 22 November, Allen commented in a letter to Pelham Warner that Copson was one of several players who did not have 'a great deal of cricket brain.' In particular he thought that Copson tried too many experimental deliveries, including his 'dapper', presumably a slower ball, which was often hit for four. Even so he still listed him as a 'possible' for the First Test. Shortly after this, however, Copson suffered a recurrence of his earlier injury, and missed the next two matches, against an Australian XI at Sydney and against Queensland at Brisbane. By now he had no performance on the field which could be set against his captain's evident lack of confidence in him.

On 4 December, England went into the First Test Match, without Copson of course, at the Woolloongabba ground at Brisbane, with the depressing record of only having won two of their seven first-class matches so far. They surprised everyone, not least themselves, by winning by the handsome margin of 322 runs. An excellent century by Maurice Leyland enabled England to take a first innings lead of 124 and, in their second innings, Australia collapsed for 58 runs on a 'sticky dog' wicket. Allen and Voce bowled unchanged to take all nine wickets to fall, McCormick being absent ill.

Bill had some more match practice in a two day friendly match against a Queensland Country XI at Ipswich but, by then, it was unlikely that he would be able to claim a place in the Test team in front of Voce. England won the next Test match even more convincingly by an innings and 22 runs, Hammond playing another superb innings, of 231. The Englishmen were jubilant, having gone two games up in the five match rubber. However they were soon brought down to reality when, in a strange third match at Melbourne, England, in reply to Australia's first innings total of 200 for 9 declared, made their own declaration at 76 for nine. This was the first time in Test cricket that both sides had declared their first innings closed. The second day's play was on a 'gluepot' wicket and thirteen wickets fell in about three hours. England had hoped to take more Australian wickets cheaply but the pitch had eased considerably and Bradman came into his own with a superb match winning innings of 270. He added 346 for the sixth wicket with J.H. Fingleton, at the time a record for any wicket in a Test match in Australia. England were set an enormous fourth innings target and, despite another splendid century from Leyland, went down by 365 runs. The match had been watched by a record crowd of 350,534, the most for any first-class game in Australia.

The tourists' itinerary in those more leisured days gave the team a well deserved break after the rigours of the Test Matches in which they visited Tasmania. Copson played in both first-class matches on the island, his first first-class match for seven weeks, taking four wickets in the first game against the state side, not of course a competitor in the Sheffield Shield at that time. He took four wickets against a Combined Tasmania XI in the second game at Hobart which was spoiled by rain and ended in a draw. Because of the imminence of the Fourth Test at Adelaide, Bill was not given a chance in the state match against South Australia which preceded it.

England went down to a heavy defeat by 148 runs in the Fourth Test. Some very effective spin bowling by Fleetwood-Smith, who had a match return of ten for 239, helped dismiss the visiting side for 330 and 243, despite a good score by Barnett of 129 in the first innings. Bradman made a rather dour 212 in 437 minutes, hitting only fourteen fours. The sides were now level at two games all in the five match rubber and all would depend on the final encounter at Melbourne.

The MCC team next played two minor matches against country sides at Geelong and Canberra. Copson played in the second of these games at Canberra, the new Australian capital city, which had been officially 'opened' as recently as 1927, by the Duke of York. It has been the custom in more recent times for English touring sides to play a Prime Minister's XI in the federal capital, but on this tour the opponents were the Southern Districts of New South Wales. Copson, 'though not working up his full pace' had great success accomplishing his best performance of the tour in taking seven wickets for 16 runs in the home team's second innings when they were dismissed for 78, with MCC winning the game very comfortably by an innings and 140 runs.

The side arrived at Ushers Hotel in Sydney for their second match against New South Wales, where they gave a most disappointing display. Devastating bowling by Lush and Chilvers dismissed the tourists for only 73 in their first innings after the home side had made 231. They were set 405 runs to win the match in the fourth innings and, although Barnett played another splendid knock of 117 and MCC reached a score of 200 for the loss of only three wickets, their final seven went down for only 99 runs. Copson took three wickets in the second New South Wales innings.

Copson was selected for the last state match of the tour, versus Victoria, but the match was badly affected by rain and ended in a draw. On an easy paced pitch, he took two wickets in a distinctly moderate spell of bowling in which he conceded sixty four runs in nineteen eight-ball overs, with no maidens. If he was to break into the side for the final Test match, Copson needed to impress in these two matches against the strongest state sides. He didn't, and so Allen, Voce and Farnes took the quick bowlers' places.

All was set now for the deciding Test Match at the Melbourne Cricket Ground. England never looked like making a contest of this game. Australia most conveniently won the toss and batted over into the third day to score 604 runs. This was then the highest innings total made by Australia against England in Australia. Centuries were scored by Bradman, McCabe and Badcock. A thunderstorm on the fourth morning of the match did not help

England and they were compelled to follow on their first innings of 239. Hardstaff was the only England player to exceed fifty. England fared even worse in their second innings and at close of play on the fourth day were 165 for eight.

On the fifth morning, twelve thousand people were admitted free to watch the remainder of the match. Only two balls were bowled, and these dismissed Voce and Farnes. England thus lost by an innings and 200 runs their largest margin of defeat by Australia to date. This was the first occasion in Test Match history where a side had recovered from being two matches down to win a rubber by three games to two. It had been an absorbing series which had been watched by a total of 954,290 people and brought to an end the era of timeless Test Matches in Australia.

It was a dispirited MCC side that left Australia for the calmer waters of New Zealand. The team had not been quite good enough to resist such a strong Australian comeback after losing their first two Tests. Their batting had let them down on many occasions. Leyland had been a success scoring two Test centuries and Voce was the most successful bowler with 26 wickets. Copson had not bowled well enough to break into the Test side. He had taken 20 wickets in first-class games but had not shown the deadly form he had displayed in England the previous summer.

The tourists sailed in the *S.S.Awatea* from Sydney Harbour on 12 March and arrived in Auckland three days later. They were to play three first-class games in New Zealand but no Test Matches. Their first game was against a combined Canterbury and Otago side at Christchurch, a three day game that was ruined by rain as no play took place on the last day. Bill opened the bowling with Farnes after MCC had made 217. The home team were dismissed for 157 and he took three wickets for 26 runs in 14.4 overs. The next game, at the Basin Reserve Ground in Wellington, was billed as New Zealand v MCC, but there has always been a school of thought that this match deserved Test match status. The home team was certainly of Test match standard as it had been selected entirely from players chosen for the forthcoming tour of England in 1937. New Zealand were forced to follow on after MCC had posted 427 and in the second innings their batsmen managed to edge one run ahead of this total, but as only three minutes remained there was no time for MCC to complete a victory. Copson did not play in this game, but returned for the third match of this short tour against a combined Auckland and Wellington team at Eden Park, Auckland.

This was to be his last overseas first-class match: he was not quite twenty nine years of age and could reasonably expect to be considered for further tours, if he could maintain his form and fitness. In this match he took a further four wickets, three of them in the first innings. MCC won the game fairly easily by seven wickets.

Copson had finished the tour by heading the first-class bowling averages with the not unsatisfactory record of 27 wickets for 535 runs at an average of 19.81 in eight first-class matches. In seven minor matches he took fifteen wickets at 9.20. Although he had scarcely come near selection for the Test side, he had gained experience of bowling on Australian wickets which he probably thought would stand him well in future. *Wisden*, in fact, said he bowled well 'when he found a pitch to suit him.' Overall though, his tour was a disappointment. Only George Duckworth, the reserve wicket-keeper played in fewer first-class matches, and Copson's absences from the side, admittedly because of injury, had enabled Voce and Farnes to stake a better claim in the Test teams. His position was highlighted by a dismissive remark made by the team manager to the *News Chronicle* when the team finally returned to London. Asked why Copson had not played in any of the Tests, he simply said, 'Because he wasn't selected.'

The MCC team was now to embark on an exciting finale to their arduous tour. They were scheduled to return to England via the United States of America, thus completing their journey round the world. The tourists left Auckland on 3 April in the *S.S.Mariposa* for Los Angeles where they arrived a fortnight later, on 17 April. The team had the unforgettable experience of being shown round the Metro Goldwyn Mayer film studio at Hollywood, by special invitation, on their brief visit. The cricketers met Binnie Barnes and Eleanor Powell and had their photographs taken with various film stars. They were then taken to see filming of a scene from *The Prisoner of Zenda*, starring Ronald Colman, Madeleine Carroll and Raymond Massey. The team met C.Aubrey Smith, the veteran film actor who had emigrated to America in the 1930s and who also starred in the film. An excellent cricketer before he took up acting, he had won four Blues at Cambridge University, and played once for England when he captained R.G.Warton's side on their tour of South Africa in 1888/89, and appeared in 99 matches for Sussex between 1882 and 1896. He was a most enthusiastic expatriate who still retained his passion for the game. He ran his own

41

Hollywood cricket team, with its own specially constructed ground: a number of well known British actors played for him, including David Niven and Boris Karloff. From various accounts of their visit, the team, many of them no doubt regular cinemagoers, seem to have been highly excited by their encounter with the 'celebs' of the day.

Players as autograph hunters.
Stan Worthington, Charles Barnett and Bill Copson find themselves queueing for the signature of Douglas Fairbanks jr.
At Hollywood on the set of The Prisoner of Zenda.

After their memorable few hours in Los Angeles the team left the same evening by the Santa Fé train for Chicago, with the skipper, G.O.B.Allen, staying behind. This journey took them two and a half days. They changed trains in that city and arrived in New York in the early morning. They embarked on the *R.M.S.Queen Mary*, and travelled across the Atlantic, arriving at Southampton five days later on 26 April. The *Queen Mary* was the flagship of the Cunard White Star Line, the biggest passenger ship then afloat, and 'the last word' in luxurious ocean travel. She had made her maiden voyage to New York in May, 1936, and was now engaged in much publicised competition with the French liner *Normandie* for the fastest crossing of the Atlantic.

In spite of his disappointing performance on the cricket field, Bill Copson, from The Blocks in Stonebroom, could at least say he had touched the international highlife, albeit for what proved to be the only time in his career. For the Copsons jointly, the income from the tour, although some way below that of many other Cunard passengers, brought a notable improvement to their living standards: they had a new three-bedroomed detached house built in Bertrand Avenue, Clay Cross. Not one for inactivity, Emily Copson ran a hairdressing business from the house for some years. Their son Michael was born at this address in November, 1943.

We're on our way home.
The MCC side on board R.M.S.Queen Mary in April 1937.
Back row (l to r): T.S.Worthington, W.H.Copson, W.Ferguson (scorer), C.J.Barnett, J.M.Sims, J.Hardstaff, A.E.Fagg, K.Farnes. W.Voce.
Front row: L.E.G.Ames, M.Leyland, R.Howard (manager), R.E.S.Wyatt, W.R.Hammond, H.Verity, G.Duckworth.
For various reasons, three players, G.O.B.Allen (captain), L.B.Fishlock and R.W.V.Robins, were absent from the photograph.

*The 'official' photograph of the MCC side which toured Australia in 1936/37.
Back row (l to r): W.H.Ferguson (scorer), L.B.Fishlock, T.S.Worthington,
A.E.Fagg, J.Hardstaff, R.Howard (manager).
Middle row: T.H.Wade, H.Verity, C.J.Barnett, K.Farnes, W.H.Copson, J.M.Sims,
W.Voce.
Front row: L.E.G.Ames, W.R.Hammond, R.W.V.Robins, G.O.B.Allen (capt),
R.E.S.Wyatt, M.Leyland, G.Duckworth.*

Chapter Five

Test Cricket, At Last

In those days professional cricketers were rarely allowed much time off from their county duties. Bill and Stanley Worthington were both required to play at Old Trafford in Derbyshire's opening game of the season on 1 May, 1937, just five days after returning from their long winter's absence which did not leave very much time for any period of family reunions or rest and resuscitation from their travels.

A special ceremony was held at The Assembly Rooms, Derby on Wednesday, 5 May, to celebrate the winning of the Championship in 1936. This had been delayed until the two Australian tourists had returned. The Duke of Devonshire, President of the Club, supported by various local Mayors, presented gold wristwatches to all the competing players and expressed his great pleasure at seeing Copson and Worthington safely back from their winter endeavours. The team were also awarded bonuses related to the number of games that they had played in the Championship winning side. Bill, with 26 appearances, received £50 1s 6d (£50.07). They were also each given a silver cigarette case as a special gift from Derby County Football Club. One wonders if the Cricket Club ever reciprocated this generosity by giving the Football Club players a similar present for their successes in winning the F.A .Cup and two Football League Championships in post war years. Somehow it seems unlikely!

After their triumph in the previous summer Derbyshire lost their title to a rejuvenated Yorkshire side. They finished third in the county table, behind Yorkshire and Middlesex, although their points percentage was slightly higher than 1936. The team had a new captain in R.H.R.Buckston, an Eton-educated schoolmaster from Bournemouth, who although very popular with his team accomplished little as a batsman. The county won fourteen out of twenty eight Championship matches, losing six and drawing eight.

Copson was seriously troubled by injury this season and appeared in only sixteen of these games. His outstanding bowling performances were few and far between, but when they did occur they were little short of sensational. The first was in the match against Lancashire on 3, 4 and 5 June at Burton-on-Trent, when he performed the first hat trick of his career. He sent back Watson, Sibbles and Wilkinson in consecutive balls to restrict the visitors to a narrow first innings lead. Prior to this game he had only taken sixteen wickets in five Championship outings.

Apart from a seven-wicket match aggregate against Sussex at Horsham, he had little other success until a knee injury enforced his absence for five matches after 25 June. It was on his return that he accomplished what was, statistically, his best ever feat in first-class cricket. The occasion took place at Derby, Warwickshire being the visitors. Making the ball swing violently either way and bowling extremely fast, he demolished his opponents for 28 runs before lunch on the opening day. All the Warwickshire batsmen were helpless against him. Half the side were dismissed for eighteen runs and Copson dismissed Dollery, Fantham, Mayer and Hollies in four consecutive balls to finish with the astonishing figures of 8.2-2-11-8.[19] *Wisden* described this performance as 'Bowling probably better than at any time since his debut in 1932, he maintained great speed and made the ball swing disconcertingly either way. Batsmen compelled to make late defensive strokes were helpless against him.' Contemporary Press reports suggested that there was little wrong with the pitch to account for Copson's success. His achievement has remained the best eight-wicket return for Derbyshire in first-class cricket: in the 'official' Championship it has been bettered only five times in 108 seasons.[20]

In Warwickshire's second innings he took the wicket of Norman Kilner with his second ball, thus taking five wickets in six balls. This was the first time that this had been done in first-class cricket although three other players have subsequently equalled this feat.[21] His record was seven wickets in 18 balls, eight in 28, nine in

---

19   His ball by ball analysis was as follows: ....w./.w..../2..1../1...../1....w/.....1/ 1..w../..4.ww/ww

20   These are by D.Shackleton, 11.1-7-4-8, for Hampshire *v* Somerset, Weston-super-Mare, 1955; C.H.Palmer, 14-12-7-8, for Leicestershire *v* Surrey, Leicester, 1955; E.G.Dennett, 6-1-9-8, for Gloucestershire *v* Northamptonshire, Gloucester, 1907; G.E.Tribe, 14.2-10-9-8, for Northamptonshire *v* Yorkshire, Northampton, 1958; and D.L.Underwood, 10.1-6-9-8, for Kent *v* Sussex, Hastings, 1973.

21   This particular feat has since been achieved by W.A.Henderson for North-East Transvaal *v* Orange Free State, Bloemfontein, 1937/38; P.I.Pocock for Surrey *v* Sussex, Eastbourne, 1972, in his last two overs of the match; and Yasir Arafat for Rawalpindi *v* Faisalabad, Rawalpindi, 2004/05.

48 and ten in 53, all on the same day, a remarkable feat indeed. He took a further three wickets in this innings to finish with match figures of eleven for 93. In this match he also had success with the bat, scoring an undefeated 30, including seven fours, out of 36 for the last wicket with Tommy Mitchell. Derbyshire won this game comfortably within two days.

He had a further five wickets in an innings against Essex at Ilkeston at the end of July, but then missed four further games through injury. Rest seemed to do him good, and as with his previous absence, he returned to take another eight wickets in an innings. In the match against Sussex at Derby, bowling on a rain-affected pitch, he had the impressive figures of eight for 64.[22] Thanks to a superb score of 238 from Stanley Worthington, who retired hurt through cramp, Derbyshire defeated the visitors very easily by nine wickets.

All in all, Copson, apart from his occasional flashes of exceptional bowling, had for him a somewhat disappointing season, although he had missed a number of matches because of injuries. His elevation to Test match status seemed to still be somewhat distant. Fast bowlers selected for the three Test Matches against the visiting New Zealand side included Gover (another successful season with 201 wickets), Voce, Jim Smith, Wellard and Austin Matthews. If Bill had struck anything like his form of the previous summer and shown more consistency in his performances, he would surely have received preference over any of these last three.

For Derbyshire, the advance of George Pope was most pleasing. He had played only a small part in the Championship success the previous season because of injury. In 1937 he narrowly missed completing the cricketer's double and scored three centuries. Tommy Mitchell, like Copson, was troubled by injury, when he broke his wrist. At the end of the season the county club arranged for Copson to undergo a thorough medical examination because he was too valuable a commodity to lose regularly through injury. The results, however, seem to have been inconclusive.

* * * * *

---

22   Copson had rather more success at Derby than Chesterfield. He played 46 first-class matches at Derby, taking 248 wickets at 15.28, with five wickets in an innings sixteen times. At Chesterfield in 45 matches he took only 153 wickets at 20.32, with only six five-wicket returns.

The visit of the Australians in 1938 might have provided a further opportunity for Bill to show his mettle on the wider stage, but this was not to be. Derbyshire slipped further down the county table this season, finishing in fifth position. Yorkshire were champions for the second successive year, winning no fewer than twenty of their twenty eight matches at the superior average of 9.14 points per match. Derbyshire's record was an average of 6.40 points from twenty eight games played, with eleven victories. They drew only six matches but went down to defeat eight times.

Bill Copson sets off with Albert Alderman and Denis Smith
to net practice at the start of the 1938 season.
He has the ball: they have the thigh pads.

Bill Copson had a more satisfactory season and enjoyed much better health than the previous summer. He played in twenty three Championship games and took 101 wickets. He captured five or more wickets in an innings on eight occasions, though without taking as many as ten in any match. He did not come anywhere near selection for any representative match, although his county colleague George Pope, who had another excellent season, played in the Test Trial and was among those chosen to attend for the First Test at Trent Bridge without making his debut, for which he had to wait until after the war.

His best performance was in the game against Nottinghamshire at Ilkeston, where he had a fine spell in the second innings, taking seven wickets for fifty nine runs when the county were dismissed for 204 runs. The home team knocked off the 207 runs required for victory for the loss of only one wicket. He had also played his part as a batsman in this match as he came to the wicket in his usual position as last man when the county still required 41 runs for a first innings lead. He helped Harry Elliott, the wicket-keeper, to add 40 runs for the tenth wicket to level the scores, of which he made four.

He had another good return in the very next match against Warwickshire at Edgbaston, a game set aside for G.A.E.Paine's benefit. Bill did not do him many favours however as he dismissed him in both innings for a pair! The convention of giving the beneficiary one run off the mark it would appear was not honoured for some reason. Copson took four Warwickshire second innings wickets for five runs on the last morning to finish with six for 36 and a match return of nine for 76. Derbyshire won by an innings.

He had two more impressive performances before the end of the season. Derbyshire easily overcame Worcestershire at Derby, when Bill had another inspired spell in the visitors' second innings with four wickets for eleven runs to finish six for 38 and nine in the match. Again in the very next match he bowled well to take five Nottinghamshire first innings wickets including the first three batsmen for only thirteen runs.

He had ended his seventh first-class English season with an aggregate of 662 wickets at an average of 18.24. Although he had accomplished some excellent performances and impressed a number of people with his very hostile bowling, there was a general feeling that he was injury prone and perhaps lacked the stamina to perform effectively at a higher level. Although he was just under six feet tall, his somewhat under-nourished upbringing had not given him the extra strength and build that was required of a top class bowler. His performances this summer did not bring him anywhere near consideration for the winter tour to South

Africa. Although England won that rubber by one match to nil, with four drawn games drawn, their fast bowling in this high scoring series was not particularly effective, being entrusted to Farnes, Edrich, Hammond and Perks, who between them only took 27 wickets in the Tests. Copson might well have found the hard South African wickets to his advantage had he been selected.

* * * * *

Copson finally fulfilled his ambition of becoming a Test cricketer in the season of 1939. He had a much better season than his two previous ones and turned in a number of excellent performances. His final tally of first-class wickets was 146, second only to his 160 in 1936. Derbyshire, however, had a much less satisfactory summer and for the first time since 1933 failed to finish in the top six in the Championship table, falling to ninth position. They won ten out of twenty eight games, losing eight and drawing ten, of which three failed to reach a first innings decision. The low point of the season was their dismissal for 20 by Yorkshire at Bramall Lane, Sheffield. This was the county's lowest ever innings total in the 'official' championship. Their batting consistently let them down and only six centuries were scored during the whole season.

Copson made the very wise move of starting his season with impressive figures which brought him to the notice of the Test selectors fairly quickly. In Derbyshire's first match of the season, versus Oxford University in The Parks, he performed the third and final hat trick of his career, when he dismissed the last four second innings batsmen in five balls. His match return, with five wickets in each innings, was ten for 21 in only 10.7 eight-ball overs. *Wisden* reported that 'he swung the ball and his off break was unplayable.' He also helped to add fifty runs for the tenth wicket with Rhodes. On the second day, nineteen wickets fell for eighty six runs and Derbyshire won comfortably by 163 runs at 2.45 pm. He took his third consecutive five wickets in an innings in the next match, against Surrey at Chesterfield, at one time having a spell of four for nineteen in four overs. Further successes followed and by 9 June, he had taken 48 wickets and was bowling at the top of his form. Derbyshire's next match, on 10 June, was against the West Indies touring team. In those days county games against the tourists were the highlight of the season and good performances by local players were usually the subject of much Press attention. Copson certainly made the very best of his opportunities on this occasion and had figures of six for 73 in the first innings and four for 19 in the second. Derbyshire had a comfortable first innings lead of 45 and, in the visitors' second venture, caused a sudden collapse by taking four wickets in twenty nine balls, reducing the side to 20 for five. A delay of forty minutes through bad light left the match drawn with the West Indians on 54 for six, still needing a further 96 runs to win. In this match Derbyshire fielded all three of the Pope brothers, Alfred Vardy, George Henry and Harold, the last occasion on which three brothers played in the same side in English first-class cricket.

Copson's excellent bowling in this match had increased his prospect of Test Match selection considerably and it was no surprise when this was confirmed and he was duly chosen for the First Test at Lord's due to begin on 24 June. This was a three-match series of three-day matches. The West Indians, who had been granted Test match status some eleven years previously in 1928, were captained by R.S.Grant and were at that time not the strong Test side that they became in the immediate post war years and later. The England side was a strong one, fresh from their successful tour of South Africa in the previous winter. They were captained by Walter Hammond, still very much at the height of his considerable batting powers. The remainder of the team consisted of Hutton, Gimblett, Paynter, Denis Compton, Hardstaff, Arthur Wood, Wright, Verity, Bowes and Copson. Bill was the only Test debutant.

Bowes and Copson opened the England bowling when West Indies, who had won the toss, batted first. Despite rather poor light and an extremely cold wind they did not lose their second wicket until their score had reached 147. Copson took his first Test wicket when he had the West Indian captain well taken, left-handed, by Compton at forward short leg. An excellent innings by George Headley helped to raise the West Indian score to 226 for the loss of four wickets by the tea interval. Copson also dismissed K.H.Weekes, having him caught by Gimblett. After the tea interval, Copson had immediate success when the new ball was taken when George Headley was caught at the wicket for 106. He had played a careful and most watchful innings in which he was not prepared to take any risks, but displayed a good array of his exceptional powers. Bill also took the wickets of Constantine and Martindale, both leg before wicket and finished with the highly satisfactory figures of five for 85 from 24 eight-ball overs. West Indies had been dismissed for 277. Copson had thus made an excellent start to his Test career and this performance has entitled him to a place on the Lord's dressing room honours board.

England, after being 11 for no wicket on the Saturday evening, made rapid progress on the second day and took their reply by the close of play to 404 for the loss of five wickets. After losing their first three wickets for 147, England's bright young performers Compton and Hutton added a glorious 248 runs for the fourth wicket. Both completed excellent centuries. Hammond declared overnight and Copson was immediately among the wickets again. He dismissed Stollmeyer without a run on the board when he was well caught by Verity in the gully. Headley batted well again and completed his second century of the match, 107. Copson dismissed a further three batsmen, having Sealy and Hylton caught, and then enticed Clarke to give him a return catch. England scored the 99 runs needed for victory in an hour and a quarter to give them a very comfortable victory by eight wickets.

Bill Copson could look back with extreme satisfaction on his first Test Match. To take nine wickets on debut is a comparatively rare feat.[23] What is more, this had been done at cricket's headquarters. He was still only 31 years of age and could, if he maintained this sort of form, look forward to a bright future at the international level. Sir Pelham Warner in his popular book 'Cricket Between Two Wars', published in 1942, had this to say about Copson's bowling: 'This was Copson's first Test Match and well indeed he did. He has a smooth, and not long, run to the crease, an easy action with a good follow through, and makes pace off the ground. He bowls a genuine off-break, as opposed to an in-swinger and puts life and venom into every ball. He also fielded extremely well at short leg and mid on.'

On returning the following day to the county side for the next Championship fixture, against Essex at Chesterfield, he had further success with ten wickets in the match. He and Alf Pope dismissed their opponents for 143 runs, with Bill taking 6 for 57. The home team took a first innings lead of 71 and then Essex collapsed at the start of their second innings losing their first four

---

23   There have been 27 instances in all Test cricket. For England, it has been achieved eleven times altogether, by F.Martin, T.Richardson, C.S.Marriott, K.Farnes, A.V.Bedser, J.C.Laker, R.Berry, L.J.Coldwell, J.D.F. Larter, and J.K.Lever, as well as Copson.

wickets for only five runs, two each to Alf Pope and Copson. They were all out for 117, giving Derbyshire an easy two-day win by ten wickets.

Bill Copson's splendid Test debut earned him selection for Players *v* Gentlemen at Lord's, his second and final appearance in this historic fixture. The Players' team was captained by Eddie Paynter and Bill's county colleague George Pope was also in the side, the only time he ever played in this match. The Players scored 270 in their first innings, with Tom Dollery making the top score with 70. Copson opened the Players' bowling with Bowes, as they had done in the Test match. He took the wickets of H.T.Bartlett, B.H.Valentine and F.R.Brown to finish with the useful figures of three for 49 from 20 overs. After rain had interrupted play on the second day, the Gentlemen declared their first innings some 112 runs behind. The Players, after Hutton and Compton had put on 141 in 80 minutes, declared setting their opponents 315 runs to win, but good bowling, in which the wickets were shared by four different bowlers, with two to Copson, removed any possibility of the target being reached. The Gentlemen were all out for 154: only eight wickets fell as R.E.S.Wyatt retired hurt – he later described the bowling of both Bowes and Copson in this innings as 'vicious'[24] – and J.W.A.Stephenson was absent because of a hand injury. Australian-made balls, said to be harder than those in regular use, were employed in this match: the experiment seems not to have been prolonged, perhaps because of the damage done to the performers.

Copson was never anything but an automatic selection for the Second Test to be played at Old Trafford. England made two changes, bringing in Fagg and Goddard in place of Gimblett and Verity. In the meantime Bill had four Championship matches to play before this event. He did not however obtain much bowling practice in three of these games as they were badly affected by the weather. He bowled fifteen overs at Trent Bridge without taking a wicket in a match reduced to two days by rain. He did not get onto the field in the local 'Derby' against Yorkshire at Chesterfield, where play was restricted to 100 minutes, or at Dudley in the Worcestershire fixture where only Derbyshire batted in the one

---

24 Copson was dangerous in other matches, too. Dr N.Vere Hodge, who scored 81 for Essex against Derbyshire at Ilkeston in 1937, said of Copson's bowling on that occasion, 'that really was at one's head.' Unwise perhaps, as Essex had Farnes who could respond in a similar style.

Copson's only Test Match at Lord's.
The England side going on to the field against the West Indies in June, 1939.
The front players are H.Gimblett, W.H.Copson, L.Hutton, W.E.Bowes and
W.R.Hammond (capt).

The Players side at Lord's in July, 1939.
From l to r: D.C.S.Compton, D.V.P.Wright, W.H.Copson, J.Hardstaff,
H.E.Dollery, L.Hutton, G.H.Pope, E.Paynter (capt), H.Gimblett,
W.E.Bowes, W.F.F.Price (wk).

full day's play possible. He did however have considerable success in the fourth of these matches where Derbyshire had a most emphatic win against Middlesex at Derby. Copson and Alfred Pope, bowling unchanged, dismissed them for 76 runs in their second innings. Bill took the first five wickets to fall for a mere five runs, dismissing the strong county quintet of Robertson, Brown, Edrich, Compton and Allen. This was some feat. Derbyshire completed their victory in two days: Copson's final analysis in the innings was 11-2-39-7.

It was not to be expected that Bill would reach the heights of his debut Test match, but in a rain ruined game he bowled twelve overs to take three wickets in the two West Indian innings. Only thirty five minutes' play was possible on the opening day when England, who had been sent in to bat, scored eleven runs without loss. Further interruptions occurred on the second morning and after lunch England collapsed. Hammond declared at 164 for seven, after a fighting innings of 76 by Hardstaff, who shared a fifth-wicket partnership of 88 runs with Wood. Some excellent bowling by Bowes, who took six West Indian wickets, enabled England to gain a first innings lead of 31 runs. Copson and Goddard each weighed in with two wickets. The last seven wickets went down for thirty seven runs. There were now only four and a half hours of play remaining and England batted somewhat cautiously, finally setting West Indies the impossible task of making 160 runs to win in seventy minutes. The match thus petered out into a draw.

Somewhat surprisingly, the selectors thought that Bill had not done quite well enough to retain his place in the Third and final Test Match which was to take place at Kennington Oval on 19, 20 and 21 August. England made four changes from the side chosen for the Old Trafford Test. Bowes and Copson were replaced by Nichols and Perks. Walter Keeton and Norman Oldfield, the latter playing in what was to be his only Test Match, came in for Fagg and Paynter. It was a high scoring match in which 1,216 runs were scored for the loss of only 23 wickets and was left drawn. England had won the three match series by one game to nil. Copson, with 12 wickets at an average of 15.41, took more wickets in the series than any other bowler English or West Indian. He also headed the England bowling averages, which was a creditable performance. He had had a long wait to gain Test Match recognition and could reasonably look forward to being selected again for England in the future.

Bill returned to the County Championship circuit for the remaining eleven Derbyshire matches. Of these games the county managed to win only three, so that they lost four places in the table. There was an exciting game versus Gloucestershire at Cheltenham when they won by one run. Copson had taken five for 45 in the home team's first innings, when he and Alfred Pope had shared the wickets in dismissing them for only 81. Bill had another good spell of bowling in the last match of the season, at the Aylestone Road ground at Leicester, when he took six wickets for 39 runs in the home side's first innings. Rain prevented any play on the last day.

The last few county matches had been played amidst a rapidly deteriorating international situation and the county programme had barely been completed before Hitler's invasion of Poland on 1 September brought all first-class cricket to a juddering halt. Play took place on only one ground on that fateful day, at Hove where Hedley Verity in what was sadly to be his last first-class match finished off the Sussex innings. He took seven wickets for nine runs to dismiss them for 33 runs. Yorkshire were already champions for the third year in succession. Little did many first-class cricketers foresee that there would be no more county cricket for any of them for a further six and a half years. By the end of the war a number of leading cricketers would have given their lives and for many more their careers would be over.

On 5 September, the Press tidied the season away by publishing the averages. They showed Copson in fourth place, taking 146 wickets at 15.32, behind Verity, Bowes and Goddard. It was his second best performance by that particular measure. Buried away on their now depleted sports pages, several newspapers also carried a terse sentence saying that 'MCC announced yesterday that the cricket tour to India had been cancelled.' Copson had not been selected for the side to tour of India in 1939/40, but nor had fifteen of the seventeen players who had played in the Tests against the West Indies during the summer. If the tour had gone ahead, there might have been as many as twelve Test debutants in the three match series.[25] Although the question is perhaps

---

25   The side contained only four players with Test experience, H.Gimblett, M.S.Nichols, A.W.Wellard and R.E.S.Wyatt, and four players who became Test players after the War, H.E.Dollery, S.C.Griffith, G.H.Pope and T.P.B.Smith.

hypothetical, we cannot now say whether the selectors thought Bill wasn't good enough for Test cricket, or whether the selectors had simply decided, in choosing an England 'second eleven', to give other quick bowlers their chance.

Chapter Six
World War Two

The Second World War had an immediate impact on the lives, careers and circumstances of so many people in different ways. R.C.Robertson-Glasgow, writing for the 1940 *Wisden* only a few months after the German invasion of Poland, commented that 'to look back on the English cricket season of 1939 is like peeping through the wrong end of a telescope.' Even in the first few months, there were few families in the country who were not affected to some degree by the upheaval caused to their everyday lives by events. Mass evacuation of children from cities and other areas, compulsory National Service, a rigidly enforced blackout system, food and fuel rationing, the curtailment of leisure and entertainment services, the drafting of civilians into specific areas of employment, and severely reduced transport services were just some of the major changes introduced in 1939, whose effects cumulated thereafter. Industry and agriculture were gradually transformed to meet the needs of national defence and to make the United Kingdom more self-sufficient. To their credit, the English cricket authorities very wisely decided that it was essential for the public to be able to continue to watch the game as much as possible in wartime, in order to maintain morale. Professional first-class cricketers were immediately affected as their contracts were all suspended. Many of them volunteered for or were conscripted into the armed services; or were directed into essential war work such as munitions.

Although the normal County Championship was obviously suspended for the duration, some counties continued to play friendly matches throughout the war. A full programme of one and occasionally two day matches was arranged at Lord's. The various leagues in the Midlands and North of England continued to function: many first-class cricketers who found themselves living or working in particular areas were readily co-opted into local teams. In the south, a British Empire XI, which played 243 matches over the six seasons 1940 to 1945, was founded by Desmond Donnelly, then an unknown nineteen year old who later became a

Member of Parliament. London Counties, who played 196 matches from 1941 to 1945 and West of England, with 38 games in 1944 and 1945 were also prominent. These sides and others kept a considerable number of Test match and other leading cricketers before the public, providing much enjoyment to 'cricket-starved' spectators.

Derbyshire played one county match on the two days of the Whitsuntide Bank Holiday weekend of 1940 against their close rivals Nottinghamshire at Trent Bridge but Bill Copson, although selected, failed to arrive, probably because of the vagaries of the wartime transport systems. The county made 239 for nine wickets, innings closed, L.F.Townsend making 69. Nottinghamshire took a first innings lead of 95 and Derbyshire in their second venture declared at 201 for 6. G.M.Lee, the former Derbyshire player who was one of the umpires, was allowed to bat in the second innings in place of Copson. The home side, set 106 runs to win, finished on 65 for the loss of one wicket.

A number of Derbyshire players, including Harold Pope, Worthington, Rhodes and Arnold Townsend were conscripted into the armed services. Bill Copson, along with his colleagues Mitchell, Alf and George Pope, Harry Elliott, Alderman, Denis Smith, and Leslie Townsend were later reported as engaged in 'work of national importance', a term which generally referred to the munitions industry.

In 1940, the summer of Dunkirk and the Battle of Britain, Bill, together with Leslie Townsend, had taken jobs with a coal merchant and haulage firm, J.H.Roper Ltd in Ripley, Derbyshire. The proprietor, Joe Roper, whose son Cyril later married Harold Larwood's daughter June, had been determined to bring success to his local team Butterley, who played in the Nottinghamshire and Derbyshire Border League. Former players for this club included the Derbyshire players James Disney and the Storer brothers William and Harry sr, who were all born in that village. Roper offered the captaincy to Townsend and Bill Copson was very soon among the wickets. His early season figures included five for 17 and six for 29 against Kimberley and Pinxton respectively. Butterley won their first eight matches, in which Copson took fifty wickets. He finished the season with the highly respectable figures of 78 wickets in 187 overs at an average of 5.19. The highlight of his season was his performance on the August Bank Holiday Monday when he took all ten Stainsby wickets for twenty runs in eight overs. Eight of his opponents were bowled and he also performed the hat trick. This was Butterley's tenth successive League victory. Butterley were frustrated in the league's knock-out competition when they lost in the semi-final on a saturated pitch which negated Copson's pace. This was at Heanor, who were assisted by W.E.G.Payton, a cleric and Cambridge Blue who later 'turned out' for Derbyshire. Although most of Copson's opposing batsmen were obviously some way below county standard, his season with this club can only be described as excellent and it had certainly kept his bowling skills in very good repair.

Early in 1941 Bill was seconded to work in Shipley, Yorkshire, a town on the northern edge of Bradford,[26] and lodged with a family called Lightowler who lived in Leyburn Grove. Emily remained in Clay Cross and continued to run her hairdressing business. Bill was very fortunate to work in an area where there was great enthusiasm and support for cricket, and was soon approached by the Bradford League club, Saltaire, whose home ground was just a couple of miles from his lodgings. The approach may not have been much of a surprise, as his Derbyshire colleague, Alf Pope had played for Saltaire in the previous season. The League, with twenty clubs in and around Bradford, arranged in two divisions, had been founded in 1903 and had a well-established tradition of the sternest competition for its league title and its knock-out trophy, the Priestley Cup. As in the First World War, the Bradford League flourished, even though clubs lost many of their regular players to the forces, because they were able to recruit Test and county cricketers living and working in the area. In the 1940 season, for example, more than twenty first-class cricketers played regularly in the league, as well as irregulars fitting in an odd game or two while on home leave. Saturday afternoon crowds at matches could often see games with two or three first-class players on each side. Saltaire itself was one of the best known and renowned Bradford League clubs, founded in 1869. Well known players who have played for the club, before or since Copson's connection, include

---

26 Directions given to people under the emergency provisions could be rather arbitrary. The reader might reasonably suspect the hand of a Derbyshire supporter behind the Civil Service decision to send Copson to a town close to Bradford. More prosaically, the Ministry of Supply opened a large new Royal Ordnance plant, making shell cases and bullets, at Steeton, near Keighley in 1941, about four miles from Shipley: at one stage of the war, it had nearly 4,000 employees.

the immortal Sydney Barnes,[27] Bill Bowes, Jim Laker, Tom Goddard, Bill Voce, Arthur Fagg, Cliff Gladwin, Willie Watson and Arthur Mitchell.

In 1941, Bill Copson assisted Saltaire, in conjunction with Alf Pope and George Wilson, who had played occasional matches for Yorkshire as an amateur, to win Division B of the League. Winning seventeen of their eighteen matches, with one drawn, the club thus gained promotion to Division A. At the time only one side, Great Horton in 1904 when they played twenty games, had won as many as seventeen league matches in a season. He also helped the club win the Priestley Cup, a knock-out competition, when after being dismissed in the final for 102, they bowled out Undercliffe for only 44. Well acquainted with playing before large crowds – this match was played before nearly eight thousand spectators at the Park Avenue ground – Copson took six for 30 and Pope four for fourteen. The side were thus unbeaten in the two competitions in this season, an achievement which has never been equalled.

Bradford League cricket.
The Saltaire side which won the Priestley Cup in 1941.
Back row (l to r): S.Crabtree, W.H.Copson, G.A.Wilson, A.V.Pope, F.Earnshaw,
H.J.Pedley, H.Ogden (scorer), J.M.Crossley.
Front row: J.C.Lee, L.F.Townsend, G.Birbeck (president), G.B.Haley (captain),
J.H.Roper (vice-president), A.Spencer.

27 Barnes took a hundred wickets for Saltaire in a season three times (including 122 at 4.10 in 1922, the League record) and twice took all ten in an innings for the club (including ten for 14 against Baildon Green in 1915, the league record until 1962) so that the club committee and its members were accustomed to getting good value for their money.

Copson's own bowling record for the year in the league from 143.3 overs was 59 wickets at an average of 6.59. Alf Pope took 69 wickets at 6.49. Unusually Bill flourished with the bat, scoring 189 runs from six completed innings with a top score of 67 not out. In a match against Great Horton, the car bringing Saltaire's Derbyshire contingent of Copson, Pope and Leslie Townsend broke down, and in their absence a promising young player, named Laker, took five wickets. George Pope and Denis Smith both appeared for Lidget Green, who played in Division A.

For the 1942 season, Bill, Alf Pope and Wilson all transferred to the Windhill club, based in Shipley, who had won Division A for the previous five seasons. They replaced the mighty Trinidadian Learie Constantine, who had moved to Liverpool, where he had a job in the Ministry of Labour dealing with the welfare of West Indians. It was reported that Constantine received a fee of £25 a match when he played for Windhill in 1940 and 1941.[28] The move by Copson and Pope set off a local controversy, and it was said that Windhill had 'poached' them. The players themselves were described as 'mercenaries.' Windhill had, though, acted within the League's rules which forbade approaches to other club's players during the season and had signed them up in October, 1941. Windhill were a wealthier club than many others in the league, and its officials were unrepentant, telling the local Press that 'If we had the League's two best bowlers in our side, we should not have let them slip away if it could have been avoided. We were within our rights in all negotiations.' Because of the crowds attracted by their matches, the clubs had suddenly become commercial entities: the Derbyshire players and, later on, the other professionals were the beneficiaries of the new circumstances. Eventually the League changed its rules to give clubs more time to negotiate with their existing professionals at the end of each season.[29]

---

28 For comparison, the average adult male wage for a manual worker in 1940 was £4/12/- (£4.60) per week.

29 It should not be thought that the clubs were overawed by the fame of their players. At the Windhill club's Annual General Meeting in 1943, the secretary Norman Bailey told the assembled company, with the Press present: 'In the past season Windhill had "nearly a team that could challenge an England side" but most had been disappointing.' Referring to players who had played in 1943 and earlier seasons he said Kippax was 'moderate to good'; Denis Smith 'very disappointing'; Ord 'very disappointing and depressed over his luck'; Constantine 'very erratic with his batting'; Ames 'very patchy and nothing like the standard we expected'; Alf Pope 'good with his batting', his bowling 'good without being destructive'; Copson both 'very brilliant and very poor'. He said of the reserve Derbyshire wicket-keeper George Beet that he 'came to us with a very strong recommendation from MCC. We were very disappointed and advised him not to make any further journeys from the Midlands.'

Copson and Alf Pope were replaced at Saltaire by George Pope, who had been invalided out of the Royal Corps of Signals with a knee injury. Copson played for Windhill for two years and then returned to the Saltaire club for the remaining two wartime seasons, 1944 and 1945. Windhill finished second in Division A in 1942, Bill taking 66 wickets at 8.42. They narrowly missed taking the title; the principal cause being their loss against Great Horton at the end of May when, fielding a side with five county players, they lost to an all amateur side by six runs. The following year he had 48 wickets at 10.39 when they again finished second.

A copy of the contract Bill signed with the club for the 1945 season shows that the club would pay William Henry Copson, now living at 30 George Street, Saltaire, the sum of six pounds per match 'in which the player shall play or be present ready to play at the request of the club. Half fees to be paid when a match is not commenced.' In his two last seasons with the club, Saltaire finished fifth in Division A in 1944 and third in 1945. Copson took 76 league wickets at 8.89 in 1944, more than any other player in the competition, and 64 at 9.43 in 1945, when Johnny Lawrence, then of Bingley and later of Somerset, was the leading wicket taker, with 69 at 6.50. The presence, no doubt brooding, of Alec Coxon in the Saltaire side in 1945 reminded Bill that when first-class cricket eventually returned, there would be stiff competition for places in county sides.

From 1941 to 1944, Derbyshire had confined themselves to two matches per season, against their immediate neighbours, Nottinghamshire. They could not however, call on any of their former professionals who were mostly fully engaged in the Bradford League. In 1945, however, with the war in Europe finally over, they made good use of the opportunity to play other counties and arranged to play as many as eight matches. Home and away fixtures with Lancashire, Leicestershire, Nottinghamshire and Yorkshire were arranged. Copson played in four of these games securing eleven wickets, but produced only one really effective spell of bowling when, 'using his best pace' in the one day match versus Lancashire at Chesterfield on 18 July, he took their last five wickets for only one run to finish with six for 25.

There can be little doubt that the Bradford League, week by week, provided the hardest competitive cricket available in Britain throughout the War. In 1943, for example, more than seventy county players appeared in its matches. Bill Copson was one of the leading practitioners in that competition, taking in his five seasons, a total of 313 wickets at 8.70. Only the Pope brothers took more wickets. All in all Copson had played a fair amount of cricket during the conflict and had kept his skills as well honed as he could, through the distinct advantage of playing against a good number of top class players.

Chapter Seven
Final First-Class Seasons

In spite of, or perhaps because much war-time austerity remained in place, there was strong sense of anticipation in the spring of 1946 among cricket followers, whose number included the author, about the return of a full season of first-class cricket, with its county championship, a touring side of players with new names, university teams and festival matches at seaside resorts. County cricket was still followed avidly by millions of people, even though Press reporting was limited by newsprint rationing. However, changes started to appear: in particular the distinctions made between amateurs and professionals began to decline.

It had been decided that the counties would each play twenty six Championship matches, so that the rankings would be decided entirely on points. This did away with the highly unpopular 'average points per match' method which had been introduced because counties played different numbers of games. Under the heading of 'rationalisation', each county was now required to play against every other county at least once, ten of the counties being met in home and away matches and the other six to be played either at home or away. It is interesting to note that Derbyshire did not first meet Middlesex in a County Championship match until 1929. Very few of their players therefore would ever have had the opportunity of playing at Lord's in a first-class match prior to that date, apart from matches against MCC from time to time or through selection for representative matches.[30]

Derbyshire resumed their season with a new captain, G.F.Hodgkinson, from a family with greengrocery businesses in the county. Robin Buckston, the 1939 captain, who served in the Forces, had been invalided out and did not feel fit enough to resume first-class cricket, although he captained the Second XI. Stanley Worthington, a professional who had been a commissioned officer in the Royal Electrical and Mechanical

---

30   For the record, Derbyshire surprisingly did not meet Oxford University until 1928 and Cambridge University until 1957.

Engineers, was made vice-captain, and led the side in nine matches. Alfred Pope, a stalwart of the pre-war team, born the same year as Copson, decided to play League cricket, which he did most successfully for Mitchells and Butlers in the Birmingham League, as their professional for four seasons. Other former players who had retired were Tommy Mitchell and Leslie Townsend. Harry Elliott had also retired, to become an umpire, although he was to be recalled briefly to play in the following season.

Bill Copson was now 38 years old and could, in accordance with the conventions of the time, reasonably expect to play for a few more seasons in the county side. As we have seen, he had maintained his skills with great success in Bradford, and now returned to live 'full-time' at Clay Cross, and was back at work with the Clay Cross Company. C.B.Fry, writing an article called 'The Bowling Problem', had this to say about him in *The Cricketer* magazine's 1946 'Spring Annual':

'How easy to forget the talent we already possess – known talent. For instance what of W.H. Copson of Derby? In England I have heard he bowls rather short. I have not noticed this myself. I have seen him bowl well and with success in Australia, but he could not in the 36-37 team displace Allen who was captain, nor Voce who is left handed, nor Farnes who was apparently more outright fast. But I am sure that if Australia had as good a medium-fast bowler (and very lively off the pitch at that) we should be hearing something of his prospective terror. Myself, I have always admired Copson's bowling and I do not know the reason of our silence about him.'

This was high praise indeed from one of this country's most respected judges of cricketers and a legendary, though perhaps eccentric, journalist of his time. It remained to be seen if Bill could measure up to the standards expected of him in the immediate post-war period.

With one of the weaker batting sides in the championship, and suffering from 'slackness of fielding' according to *Wisden*, Derbyshire had a most disappointing initial post-war summer. Often playing in cold, wet conditions, they had to wait until 5 July to record their first win of the season, a narrow two-wicket victory over Surrey at Derby. Altogether they won only five of their Championship fixtures, losing twelve and drawing the remainder, one being abandoned without a ball bowled. They were also heavily defeated in their one other first-class game, versus the Indian tourists. Copson was one of two survivors of the effective pre-war bowlers, the other being George Pope. He was ably supported by Cliff Gladwin who, in his first full season, shared the new ball with Bill on occasions and took over one hundred wickets.

Still opening the bowling, though he had a variety of partners, Copson played in twenty four Championship games and took five or more wickets in an innings on five occasions. He finished with 93 first-class wickets in the season at an average of 20.47. He did not bowl sufficiently well to be asked to play in the two Test Trial matches, despite the professed wish of the selectors to 'view' as many players as possible. Thus he did not come anywhere near selection for the Test Matches against All-India, nor was he ever a serious contender for the tour to Australia which had been arranged, at fairly short notice, for the ensuing winter. Fast bowlers chosen for the three home Tests were Bowes, Voce, Pollard and Gover. Two of these, Pollard and Voce, were chosen for Australia, together with the undoubted success of the season, Alec Bedser, who performed the exceptional feat of taking twenty two wickets in his first two Tests.

Bill did on occasions display his old fiery and hostile bowling form, notably in the match against Sussex at Abbeydale Park, Dore, a suburb of Sheffield, a new venue for the county and actually located in the neighbouring county of Yorkshire.[31] In later years Yorkshire used this ground for a number of their home games. Copson took six wickets for forty nine runs in the visitors' second innings, his best statistical return of the season.

* * * * *

The 1947 season is of course, best remembered for the exceptional batting of Denis Compton and Bill Edrich, both of whom broke the record aggregate of 3,518 runs in a season made by Tom Hayward in 1906. Compton also made eighteen first-class centuries, overtaking the sixteen made by Jack Hobbs in 1926. It was a summer of almost unbroken sunshine and attracted large numbers of spectators to the many exciting games played. It came

---

31 Dore was part of an area in the 'traditional' county of Derbyshire which was transferred to the City of Sheffield, and thence to Yorkshire, in the 1930s.

to be known as the 'vintage summer' and seems, even now, to have gone on for ever. Members of the bowling fraternity toiled under these conditions: in the Championship they conceded runs at the rate of 27.51 per wicket, a figure only once exceeded in Copson's career, and almost four runs per wicket more than in 1946.

Bill Copson had the somewhat unexpected, but well-deserved, experience of being recalled to play in the final Test of the season against South Africa at Kennington Oval. This was only the third Test Match of his career. It turned out to be his last.

Middlesex won the County Championship, the county's first success for twenty six years. Despite Test Match calls, their powerful batting scored at a tremendous rate, permitting their bowlers sufficient time to dismiss their opponents. They won nineteen out of their twenty six matches and finished ten points ahead of the runners up, Gloucestershire. Derbyshire had a much better season and rose to fifth position, the biggest positional gain by any side in the competition. They won eleven matches in all, under their new captain, E.J.Gothard. Although he accomplished very little with the bat, he had one remarkable bowling performance, against Middlesex at Derby, when he took a hat trick by dismissing Alan Fairbairn, Bill Edrich and Walter Robins. He was the second and last Derbyshire amateur to perform this feat. Prior to this game he had only taken one first-class wicket. Copson, despite missing four consecutive games in the first two weeks of June, accomplished some good performances, although only capturing five wickets in an innings on four occasions. A match he was sorry to miss was that against Somerset at Chesterfield, on 11 June, when Derbyshire completed the rare feat of defeating their opponents in a single day. This was the first occasion that this had happened in the County Championship since 1925. Somerset were dismissed for 68 and 38, George Pope taking thirteen wickets. This has remained the only instance of Derbyshire winning a first-class match in a single day's play. Of the fifteen 'one-day' Championship matches since 1890, six have involved the defeat of Somerset.

Bill Copson's selection for the final Test was surprising. The visiting South Africans had a strong batting side. After enforcing the follow on in the First Test at Trent Bridge, England made a spirited comeback in their second innings and an unlikely and courageous tenth-wicket partnership between J.W.Martin and Eric Hollies, set South Africa too big a task and they finished sixty one runs short of victory for the loss of only one wicket in their second innings. The visitors were comprehensively beaten in the next three Tests so that the result of the rubber was already decided and the last Test was therefore a 'dead' one.

England had tried an interesting variation of opening bowlers in the first four Tests. In the First Test, as we have said, J.W.Martin, in the only Test of his very short first-class career, had partnered Alec Bedser. In the second game of the series, at Lord's, the selectors tried Bill Edrich and also called up Copson's county colleague George Pope for a somewhat belated Test match debut as first change.[32] For the Third Test, at Old Trafford, Alec Bedser was rested for the first time in his then meteoric Test career. He had performed valiantly in his first two Test series in 1946 and 1946/47 and it was considered he was in some need, albeit temporarily, of a short period away from the Test match arena to recover his stamina. He and Hollies stood down, to be replaced by Test debutants Kenneth Cranston and another Derbyshire seam bowler, Cliff Gladwin. For the Fourth Test, at Headingley, Harold Butler the Nottinghamshire fast bowler, who was thirty four years of age was called up for his Test debut to replace Gladwin. He bowled very well and took seven wickets in the match, including a spell of three wickets for twelve runs in the second innings. However Butler strained a leg muscle and was suddenly unavailable for the final Test Match.

Thus it was that the Test selectors turned, at extremely short notice, to Bill Copson who had not, at the time, been bowling particularly well and had not played in a Test match since 1939. He had played in Derbyshire's Championship fixture at Scarborough, where he failed to take a wicket in the Yorkshire innings of 522, being hit for 75 runs in 18 overs. The game finished on Friday, 15 August and he then had to travel the 250 miles or so down to London ready for the start of play at 11.30 am the very next day in a Test match. For England, Jack Robertson and Reg Howorth made their Test debuts and Bill Edrich was unable to play on account of a badly strained shoulder muscle which was to prevent him bowling again during the season. This did not however stop him playing as a batsman for Middlesex in their vital Championship game at Cheltenham against Gloucestershire. This, at the time, raised a few eyebrows, particularly from their opponents! Edrich had taken 67 wickets by this stage of the summer and had he been able to bowl

---

32   It was also his only Test appearance.

for the rest of the season might well very have emulated the feat of Jim Parks sr, ten years previously, who completed the unique 'double' of 3,000 runs and 100 wickets.

For the first time ever, Derbyshire provided both opening bowlers in a Test Match as Cliff Gladwin was also playing. England won the toss and, although scoring somewhat slowly in this four day game, amassed the respectable score of 427. Copson batted for the first and only time in his Test career, scoring six runs in thirteen minutes, before being bowled by the medium pace of Ossie Dawson. N.B.F. 'Tufty' Mann, the South African slow left-arm bowler, in long economical spells, took four for 93 from 64 overs, of which 28 were maidens. Gladwin made a very useful 51 not out which made some amends for his running out of Godfrey Evans, when he refused an easy single to deep mid off. Copson had a steady spell of bowling in the South African first innings. At one stage they had reached 243 for the loss of four wickets, Bruce Mitchell being the sheet anchor. He had an inspired piece of bowling when he took the new ball at the Pavilion End and dismissed Mann, V.I.Smith and last man out Mitchell in only seven balls, without conceding a run. His figures in this spell were seven overs, six maidens, four runs, three wickets.

This was the first and only time that the author ever saw Bill Copson bowl and he remembers being impressed and surprised at how short his run was – about ten paces or so – compared with the pace he generated off the pitch. Howorth also bowled well in a very long spell and took a wicket with his first ball in Test cricket. England went for quick runs in their second innings to build on their lead of 125 and Denis Compton, at the very top of his form, made a most attractive 113. This was his fourth century of the rubber and altogether against the tourists he hit six scoring over a thousand runs at an average of 84.78. South Africa were set a total of 450 runs to win the match and came very close to achieving the target. Mitchell, in another splendid innings, completed his second hundred of the match and finished on 189 not out: he was on the field for all but eight minutes of the match. South Africa finished only 28 runs short of the required total and the match was drawn. Bill failed to take a wicket in this innings, although chances were missed off him.

This was the end of Copson's all too brief Test career, in which he finished with career figures of fifteen wickets at an average of 19.80 from three appearances, an average of five wickets per match. This is a very high figure compared with many other Test Match bowlers, but is, of course, over a very short period.

He played two more matches this season, taking nine Worcestershire wickets in Derbyshire's final Championship game and making, for him, a rare Festival appearance, this time at Kingston-upon-Thames for North versus South, when he failed to take any wickets. He finished the season with 89 first-class wickets. In the game against Essex at Chesterfield he added 62 runs for the tenth wicket with Cliff Gladwin, scoring an undefeated 38. This was his second highest individual innings in first-class cricket. This was also the match in which T.P.B.Smith of Essex, who normally batted rather higher up, scored 163 runs when batting at number eleven in the order, a world record in first-class cricket. Copson was one of six Derbyshire bowlers who toiled in very hot weather before Worthington finally captured Smith.

* * * * *

The 1948 season saw the much-awaited arrival of the Australians captained by Donald Bradman, who was making his fourth and final tour to this country. The story of their triumphant tour has often been told. The side remained unbeaten in all their matches and overwhelmed England by four games to nil in a very one sided rubber. The Australians played to packed houses at almost all their matches and generated a huge amount of interest. *The Cricketer* at one stage reported that the Australians 'liquidated county sides in a most uncompromising fashion.'

Alas, Bill had a most disappointing season: he played in only nine Championship matches and missed the county's match against the Australians at Derby. He had the misfortune to break a bone in his foot when batting in his county's first innings against Somerset at Ilkeston on 5 June. He was absent from the side for six weeks. He had accomplished only one good performance prior to that date, when he took seven for 103 in Warwickshire's first innings total of 398 in Derbyshire's first home game of the season. Although it is unlikely that he realised it at the time, the seventh of these wickets, T.L.Pritchard bowled for six early on the second day of the match, was Copson's thousandth in first-class cricket. The seven wicket return had earned him a place in the Test Trial which took place at Edgbaston on 2, 3 and 4 June, showing that the selectors were still interested in him as a possible candidate for the Test side. Copson played for The Rest and opened the bowling with Harold Butler. The match was ruined by the weather and neither side completed an innings in a game played in very miserable conditions. Copson bowled well against a strong England XI and took the wickets of Washbrook, Compton and Yardley in thirteen overs for thirty nine runs, quite a tidy performance. Nine of this side played in the First Test at Trent Bridge a week later, Robertson and Wright being replaced by Hutton and Laker, who had not played in the trial match. It is interesting to note the other members of The Rest team who must have been in the selectors' minds. These were Fishlock, Fagg, Simpson, Palmer, Emmett, Cranston, Broderick, Griffith, Robins and Butler. Only Cranston and Emmett of these players were subsequently chosen in the series, both playing in the Fourth Test at Headingley. But for his subsequent injuries, Copson might well have gained a place in one or more of the Tests as he was surely a significantly more useful and experienced bowler than the other opening bowlers used this season: Coxon, Pollard, Edrich and Watkins. The England selectors gained a reputation of being somewhat desperate men this summer, highlighted by the dramatic sacking of Hutton after the Second Test.

Copson's injury was to affect the rest of his season dramatically. On 15 and 16 July, he had a successful 'fitness trial' for the Derbyshire Second XI against their Nottinghamshire equivalents at Chersterfield, in the Minor Counties Championship – this was the only match he ever played in this competition[33] – when he took one for 15 off ten overs. He returned to full duty on 17 July and took four wickets against Sussex at Burton-on-Trent, three of them for sixteen runs in a hostile spell. After that, his season went into decline and further injury restricted him to just two more Championship appearances. He finished the summer with a mere thirty one first-class wickets, his lowest ever seasonal aggregate.

Despite all Copson's tribulations, Derbyshire had a remarkably successful season in 1948. Although finally finishing sixth in the table, they reached top position on 7 June when they defeated Somerset in two days at Ilkeston. They had then won five out of their eight games, including a most convincing victory by 301 runs over Glamorgan, the eventual champions. They made it to the top again on 20 July, when they won against Sussex by ten wickets at

---

33   There can be few players who have played in a Test trial and later in a Minor Counties match, with only a six week interval between them.

Derbyshire's side in 1948.
Back row (l to r): C.S.Elliott, D.C.Brooke-Taylor, A.F.Townsend, C.Gladwin,
A.C.Revill, F.E.Marsh, G.O.Dawkes (wk).
Front row: A.E.G.Rhodes, D.Smith, E.J.Gothard (capt), W.H.Copson, G.H.Pope.

Burton-on-Trent. Their record at this stage of the season comprised nine wins out of seventeen matches played, and there was serious talk about the repeat of the glories of 1936. Although the county maintained the leading position until 10 August, the side then fell away considerably and won only two of their last nine matches, gaining only twelve points from their last seven games.

In Copson's enforced absences, Derbyshire relied on their other fast bowlers Gladwin and George Pope. They were assisted by a new bowler Leslie Jackson, another former coalminer who had previously only played one game, in 1947. Jackson finished with sixty one wickets in sixteen matches and created an excellent first impression, just as Bill had done, way back in 1932. Because of very keen competition from the many fine bowlers England possessed in the fifties however, Jackson only ever played two Test Matches in his career, one fewer than Copson. Pope completed the double in all Championship matches, but the only other player to score over one thousand runs was Charlie Elliott. Rhodes also bowled well, taking 66 wickets in Championship matches, including two hat tricks. Copson had, perhaps, ceased to be quite the essential player he had been for ten summers.

* * * * *

Another warm summer, 1949, was to be Bill's last season in the first-class game and he was to announce his retirement at its end. He was now over forty years of age and could not expect to carry on for too much longer. He was awarded a testimonial this year in recognition of his outstanding services to the county and the fact that he was approaching the end of his career.[34] Copson was one of only four survivors of the 1936 side still playing, the others being Denis Smith, Arnold Townsend and Charlie Elliott. He received a total of £2,500, worth at 2008 values some £65,000. Although this amount seems small compared to the vast sums of money received by today's very well paid top cricketers, it should be remembered that Derbyshire have always been one of the less financially well off counties, with a much smaller membership than the majority of clubs. Copson's testimonial was, at the time, the highest in the county's history, although it did not compare very favourably with other 1949 beneficiaries, such as Denis Compton, £12,200; Dick Pollard, £8,500;Tom Dollery, £6,362; and Eddie Watts £5,000. Above all else though, it gave him a degree of financial security unknown to earlier Copsons. Shortly after this, the family purchased and moved to 59, The Broadleys at Clay Cross, a small general provisions shop with living accommodation above it, Emily having kept up her interest in shopkeeping over the years. Perhaps they were concerned that Bill's income would fall once he had left first-class cricket, and thought this would be a way of hedging against this.

Bill had an injury free last season which was highly unusual for him. He appeared in all but one of Derbyshire's Championship games, regularly opened the bowling and took sixty three wickets. However he managed to take five wickets in an innings on only three occasions, with five for 34 against Somerset at Taunton the best of these, where he had a match return of eight for 48.

---

34 It was not Derbyshire's practice at this time to reward leading professionals with a 'benefit', which usually gave players the opportunity of receiving the net gate receipts from a specific match. In 1947, Denis Smith, in his thirteenth full season with the county had a testimonial worth £1,970, and A.E.Alderman received £1,659 in 1948, after he had played regularly for thirteen seasons, although he played only seven matches in his testimonial year. Copson was perhaps older than many modern beneficiaries, but Derbyshire seem to have been treated him equitably by the standards of the time.

A modest living.
Bill Copson's Clay Cross home for many years, 59 The Broadleys, is the left
hand end of this white painted terrace.
A shop in his time, it is now a vet's practice.

With the weakest batting of any of the counties, Derbyshire had a poor season and slipped to fifteenth position in the Championship. John Shawcroft later wrote that 'on the hard dry pitches of the parched summer . . . Derbyshire sometimes wore a jaded look.' They had a new captain, David Skinner, who, though maintaining the amateur tradition, had played in only one first-class match before taking up the position.[35] He was therefore the fifth county captain under whom Copson served in his twelve seasons with the team. Derbyshire only won six of their Championship games. They won their two opening matches, but did not taste victory again until 28 June. After defeating Somerset at Taunton very comfortably by an innings in two days for their fifth victory on 20 July, they then went a further nine games without a win until their last outing of the season when they again had another handsome two day innings victory, this time against Essex, at Burton-on-Trent. In this match, Copson, Gladwin and Jackson bowled out their opponents twice in a day.

---

35 He was the younger brother of Alan Skinner, who had played 83 games for Derbyshire between 1931 and 1938, captaining the side in 28 of them.

Les Jackson and Gladwin again bowled well and both appeared for England against New Zealand. The county badly missed George Pope who had asked to be released from his contract on account of his wife's serious illness. Gladwin narrowly missed the 'double' just failing to reach a thousand runs. Generally the Derbyshire batting disappointed during the whole of the summer. Copson's last match of the season was again for North versus South at Kingston-upon-Thames.

* * * * *

Copson, at the age of 41, had now officially retired from the first-class game and it was announced that he would play in the Bradford League for Lidget Green in 1950. He had taken a post as a fitter in the Plant Maintenance Department with the Clay Cross Company, which as we have seen was owned and controlled by the Jackson family, who still had strong connections with the Derbyshire club.[36] He also helped out temporarily as county coach this season for a period. Derbyshire, with Les Jackson and Gladwin opening the bowling, had a much more satisfactory summer and finished fifth in the county table.

Bill was free to play cricket on Saturday afternoons, which involved driving to Bradford and back from his home in Clay Cross, a round trip of ninety miles in weekend traffic, along ordinary roads through towns and villages. He was recalled by Derbyshire to play one midweek first-class match this year, when Leslie Jackson was playing in the famous Test Trial at Bradford, in which Jim Laker performed his exceptional bowling of taking eight wickets for two runs. Copson, in his last ever first-class match, took two wickets in the game, versus Leicestershire at Grace Road, Leicester, with his final wicket being Charles Palmer, the home side captain, caught by George Dawkes behind the stumps for 22. His last innings as a batsman was a modest nought not out, the thirty first such score in his first-class career.

---

36   Michael Copson says that 'whenever his father was required on cricketing duties, either as a player or an umpire, there was always a job for him at the Clay Cross Company when the season ended.'

Chapter Eight
Umpiring and Retirement

Bill was now retired from the first-class game and freed from travelling and the other less appealing aspects of the county circuit. He wanted to be able to enjoy a more relaxed form of the game which no doubt brought back memories of his wartime experiences playing in the Bradford League, still flourishing, though it no longer counted in dozens its players with first-class experience.

Lidget Green was a well established Bradford League club and one of the founder members in 1903: in 1949, though, it had finished at the foot of Division Two.[37] Bill played for this team as a professional from 1950 to 1956 and accomplished some excellent bowling performances. In 1950, although unable to lift the side off the bottom of the table, he took thirty eight wickets at an average of 17.05. His best performance was five for 37 versus Keighley. In 1951 he was second in the League bowling averages with five for 30 against Farsley as a highlight. The 1952 season saw Lidget Green become champions of Division Two of the League and Bill was top of the bowling averages and from 1953 onwards he helped keep the club in the top half of Division One. In 1954 he performed the hat trick when he captured six Idle wickets for twenty eight runs. Other remarkable feats this season included seven for 42 and six for 18 against Queensbury and Great Horton respectively. In the following summer he headed the League bowling averages, obtaining his best seasonal ever figures with 88 wickets at an average of 8.52 runs each. His last season in 1956 opened sensationally on 21 April when he took six wickets for three runs in helping to dismiss Brighouse for a mere 18 runs. He finished the year by heading the bowling averages again with 42 wickets at 9.89.

Bill's powers were certainly not on the wane, albeit he was no longer playing top class cricket, but at forty eight years of age he

---

37   The club withdrew from the league part way through the 2000 season.

Local celebrities.
Bill Copson and Eddie Shimwell in 1953, with the FA Cup.
Shimwell, from Birchover, near Matlock, played right-back for Blackpool in the
'Matthews final' at Wembley in that year.

no doubt felt it high time to 'hang up his boots.' He decided that cricket having been his life for so long that he would apply to become a first-class umpire. This was and still is a most sought after job for former first-class cricketers. Bill passed the rigorous examination required and joined the county umpire circuit in 1958, when Dick Coleman of Leicestershire dropped out.[38] He had arranged to take leave without pay from his job for the summer months. The other newcomer to start with him was J.B.Bowes, the former Lancashire pace bowler.

Comparatively little has ever been written about this very important branch of the first-class game. Umpires have a most demanding job and work extremely long hours of duty each day as

---

38 He stood in a three-day match, not first-class, between Derbyshire and RAF on 15, 16 and 17 May, 1957, which may have been for him a 'dry run' of some kind.

they do not obviously have the time away from the field of play that players do. Physical fitness and good eyesight are obviously very important factors. On the list of twenty three umpires which Bill Copson joined this season, there were two of his former county colleagues, Harry and Charlie Elliott. A.E.G.Rhodes was to join the list in 1959. George Pope joined the first-class list later, in 1966. Umpires at this period were chosen by the seventeen first-class county captains and reports on their performances were made by them after each match. Bill's first game was at Edgbaston on 10, 12 and 13 May when he partnered Emrys Davies, the well known Glamorgan all-rounder, in the championship match between Warwickshire and Sussex.

Altogether Bill officiated in 241 first-class matches, and after the start of the Gillette Cup in 1963, ten inter-county limited-overs matches.[39] Typically his workload comprised of twenty four first-class matches in a season, most of them in the county championship, with an occasional University or tourist game. The duties at the time included overseeing the progress of the match in accordance with the Laws of the Game and the Notes about the Laws, securing compliance with the regulations for first-class cricket, and securing compliance with regulations for drying the pitch and ground. Umpires were not at that time permitted to stand in any matches involving their former counties, so that Bill Copson's games were in effect almost always away from home, driving his Austin A55 Cambridge from one ground to the next. First-class matches were, at that time, of three days duration, so that three or four times a year he umpired two matches 'back to back' in a week at the same venue. He was never selected to stand in a representative or festival match and never reached the pinnacle of selection as a Test umpire, though he stood occasionally in the popular International Cavaliers matches. He had a reputation as an umpire who fully understood the ups and downs of both Test and county cricket, which players appreciated. Tony Brown and other first-class players have said he made his decisions calmly and firmly, without any sense of being officious or obtrusive: he had a sense of fair play. He was regarded as a quiet, but capable and straightforward umpire, though perhaps not quite in the top flight. When he eventually retired in 1967 after

---

39   In matches now designated as List A. He also stood in the experimental Midland Counties competition, arranged by the Leicestershire club at the start of the 1962 season, from which the limited overs 'formula' was developed.

ten happy years in the job he was presented with a tankard signed by all the other first-class umpires.[40]

Home from umpiring.
Bill Copson parking his car at the back of the family's shop in Clay Cross.

The only mark of controversy in his umpiring career occurred in 1960, his third season as an umpire, in the South Africans' match against Nottinghamshire at Trent Bridge. Copson and T.J.Bartley no balled the South African bowler Geoff Griffin fifteen times, eight for throwing and seven for dragging. The whole question of

---

40 Bill Copson also played a part in the well-known incident in a game at Canterbury between Kent and Hampshire on August Bank Holiday in 1963, with a BBC radio commentary by Peter West and E.W.Swanton, who was inclined to conduct himself as the sole guardian of 'The Game' and its high principles. Peter Richardson, the Kent opening bat and Colin Ingleby-McKenzie, Hampshire's captain decided 'to set up' Swanton. On a signal from West in the commentary box, they persuaded Copson – at first reluctant – to walk across the outfield towards the box to complain that 'the booming noise', from the full flow of Swanton's commentary, was distracting the batsmen. Swanton told the radio audience that he couldn't make out what was happening. By then Copson had reached the boundary and called out, 'The batsmen are complaining about a loud booming noise. Can you please stop.' Swanton said to West, 'What booming noise? I don't know what they mean.' West then told him, 'It's you they are complaining about; it's the sound of your voice.' Swanton was unamused and sent a sharply worded note to Richardson, but our subject escaped unscathed.

Griffin's bowling action attracted a huge amount of publicity in the first half of the season.[41] Despite the assistance he received from Alfred Gover at his Indoor Cricket School at Wandsworth in London, this was not satisfactorily resolved and matters came to a head in the Lord's Test Match when he was called eleven times by Frank Lee, all from the square leg position. Curiously Griffin had also taken a hat trick in this innings, the only one ever performed in a Lord's Test. After this he did not bowl again on the tour.

Bill's last first-class match was that between Warwickshire and Somerset at Edgbaston, two weeks before the end of the 1967 season, when he stood with Peter Wight, whose own umpiring career went on until 1995. By deciding not to apply to join the umpires' list for 1968, Bill thus made a clean break with first-class cricket at the age of 59 and settled down to enjoy the remainder of his life in Clay Cross where he lived at 59 The Broadleys. He continued with his job at the Clay Cross Company: no doubt he would have been looking forward to his retirement.

His son Michael married in 1968 and had moved to Gloucestershire early in 1971. On 13 September, Bill had gone to work as usual, when he complained of feeling unwell. He was brought home, where he died within the hour, of an aneurysm of the aorta. He was 63. His devoted wife Emily was by his side. The funeral service was held at the parish church of St. Bartholomew's, Clay Cross on 17 September and he was cremated at Brimington, just outside Chesterfield. In his will he left the sum of £5,016, worth now just over £62,000 according to the retail price index for 2008. Sadly Emily Copson was diagnosed with cancer shortly after Bill's death, and she died in December 1972, only fifteen months after her husband. Michael Copson had a son, Nicholas, born at Cheltenham in 1975, but he never met his paternal grandparents.

There were many tributes paid to Bill Copson in local newspapers. Many of these concentrated on the story of his introduction to the game in 1926. In the opinion of his son Michael, one of the most moving, which spoke more of his personality, was by John Twells of the Raymond News Agency which appeared in *The Derby Trader*, an odd place for Cardus-style reminiscence. He described his thoughts after he 'bumped into' Copson in the street:

---

41   Griffin had previously been no-balled in matches in South Africa, while playing for Natal.

The last time I saw Bill he was locking his car up on a park where St Alkmund's Way now runs. He was on his way down from the north for jury service at Derbyshire Quarter Sessions and no doubt spent the next week listening gravely to improbable explanations of why some youths discovered at midnight in Staveley Co-op hadn't really been shop breaking.

He was lucky if that was the worst he heard. But it wouldn't have made any difference to him. The long face, with its deeply furrowed jowls and the little blue pittings on the pale skin where the coal dust was embedded, would have remained impassive whatever the case. It always did. Bill always got on with the job – and never took long about it.

Twells went on to describe a moment in a pre-war match[42] between Derbyshire and Warwickshire:

'But as a bowler . . . or as boweller as they said in Derbyshire then. Yes. A boweller, a de-gutter. Derby. Bank Holiday. Hot day. Derbyshire pressing for the championship and Warwickshire to bat before 10,000 pressing hard upon the boundary. The tension on. Croome and Santall to open. The blond snowy hair and the rosy cheeks. And a silence all round the ground much as a Wimbledon crowd quietens down before a service and Copson, ball in hand, shamble shuffles back to bowl, kicking his toe caps outwards as he goes. He turns, guard is given and a lonely Eldritch voice deep in the square leg crowd screeches up in the silence, 'Bowell bugger, Bill.' And Bill Copson, all fiery hair and slinging arms burns past the umpire and the middle stump, a haft first javelin, sails towards wicket-keeper Harry Elliott, standing it seems in memory, halfway to the boundary. The silence explodes.'

Of his batting Twells recalled what he called 'an unlikely story', as follows[43]:

'Yes, except that it is of one stroke, against Nottinghamshire at Ilkeston. A blow, a kind of chopping shot off the back foot never before or subsequently seen, which with a cross bat, suddenly lifted a ball over the bowler's sightscreen and the

---

42   It has not been possible to identify a match with all the features described by the author.

43   This was almost certainly the match between Derbyshire and Nottinghamshire at Ilkeston in 1947, where Copson scored 22* in his side's first innings.

road on top of the bank behind. Cross bat, back foot, straight six . . . the knowledgeable will understand.'

Finally, he recalled his partisan response to an incident in a Test match[44] in 1939 about Copson's fielding:

'I recall the hatred with which I listened to the pre-war Test commentary on the radio, when there was a constant applause for fine fielding under the pavilion rails and at length the commentator said, 'Oh yes, that was another fine cut off and throw.' Yes, it was Bill of course, not getting his fair share of publicity as usual and, if my hatred for the supercilious Southerner who was commentating, could have been transmitted back over the ether, Howard Marshall would have been fatally fused to his microphone.'

* * * * *

How should William Henry Copson be rated overall as a bowler? He was one of a considerable number of first-class cricketers whose careers were very severely affected by the Second World War. He had been a late starter in county cricket, at the age of 24. He was thirty one years of age in 1939 and had overcome a number of injury problems to gain Test match status that summer. It is highly likely that he would have gained more Test match recognition in the following seasons and very possibly been selected for a second tour to Australia which was scheduled for the winter of 1940/41. He always caused batsmen a great deal of trouble with his deceptive pace off the pitch and was at his best when used in short spells. It was not often that his bowling was collared.

Bill was five feet eleven and a half inches tall and had a wiry supple frame. He was a man of very few words, quietly spoken and certainly not a person ever to talk much about himself: 'not particularly forthcoming' one fellow player said. Like many of his generation and background, he instinctively withdrew from any action which seemed to be self-promotion. This can best be seen in an incident at Saltaire in August 1944, where he rescued a four year old boy who had fallen into the Leeds and Liverpool Canal. 'He slid into the water and supporting himself on the bank with one

---

44   Probably the Lord's Test match against the West Indies in 1939, Bill's first, when P.F.Warner praised his fielding.

hand, lifted the child onto the bank with the other. He climbed out onto the bank and went away. It was all over in a few seconds.' Other youngsters who were with the child 'gazed on the retreating form of the rescuer' with amazement. The incident was seen by an office worker looking out of a window in a nearby mill who recognised Copson and told the local Press.

On the cricket field, he produced many effective and match-winning spells of bowling. He was an active fieldsman and not one to complain about his aches and pains. The part that he played in Derbyshire's championship trophy win in 1936 was considerable and it is fair to say that the team could not have achieved this success without his considerable contributions throughout that season. Donald Carr says that he was always popular with his fellow county players and was an excellent team man, never criticising others openly and rarely complaining about his own circumstances.

In his early years with Derbyshire he had suffered a fair amount of back trouble, but the County Club went to great lengths to have this remedied by sending him to various specialists. Because of the war intervention he played in a total of only twelve first-class seasons; eight from 1932 to 1939 and a further four from 1946 to 1949, plus one match in 1950. His overall career bowling record was impressive: 1,094 wickets at an average of 18.96 runs in 279 first-class matches. After his successful Test Match debut in 1939 he was very unlucky to have been dropped from the side after just two appearances. Although appearing in a Test Trial in 1948 he was never to play in Test matches again. As a tail end batsman he did not often get much chance to display any batting ability, nor was he expected to shine. E.W.Swanton once sternly described his batting as 'low in the rabbit class.' He did, though, take part in three fifty partnerships in his career, all for the tenth wicket, with a highest score of forty three made in his second season in the first-class game. These batting performances no doubt gave him much pleasure and amusement.

We may perhaps place him as one of a group of four Derbyshire pace bowlers of his time whose talents received insufficient Test recognition. The others are Les Jackson, who famously played only twice for England; Cliff Gladwin eight, though five were overseas; and George Pope, just once. It may fairly be said of all these that, if they had played for a more 'fashionable' county than Derbyshire, then they might well have made many more Test Match appearances. It is true that Copson's total number of first-class wickets fell well short of the achievements of Jackson and Gladwin, but he took his wickets more frequently at one per 47 balls, compared with one per 48 for Jackson and one per 49 for Gladwin. He was slightly more expensive at 18.96 a wicket, with Jackson on 17.36 and Gladwin on 18.30. All in all, not much to choose between them, you might say. He was, though, a rather 'straighter' bowler than these Derbyshire colleagues, taking exactly six hundred (55%) of his first-class wickets either bowled or leg before wicket. George Pope secured 54% of his wickets by these means, Les Jackson 49% and Cliff Gladwin 37%.

In Copson's twelve full seasons with Derbyshire, the county finished in the lower half of the Championship table only twice. Since Copson's retirement from regular play in August 1949, Derbyshire have finished in the lower half of the Championship table (or in more recent years, its Division Two) in 32 of 58 seasons. The county has won limited overs competitions, where Copson would perhaps have excelled, only three times. So the four consecutive seasons in the 1930s, when Derbyshire finished in the top three of the Championship, with Copson taking the new ball, are contrasted with the county's more recent struggle.

Unlike Jackson, Gladwin and Pope though, Copson can point to his performances in 1936, as the leading bowler in a team of local players who brought the County Championship to Derbyshire, as his crowning achievement. Perhaps that, something of more than miner interest, is how he should be best remembered.

Acknowledgements

First and foremost I must thank Bill Copson's son Michael, who provided a vast amount of background on his father's life and many of the splendid photographs reproduced in the book, all from his family collection. Bert Cosford, a relative by marriage, gave me many details of the Copson family tree. My thanks also go to David Baggett, a former editor of the Derbyshire Year Book and the county statistician, who was able to answer a number of questions which I put to him with his usual alacrity. Geoff Porter, Secretary of Saltaire Cricket Club, also gave me most useful information on Copson's wartime matches for that club. Jeff Driver, Chairman of Saltaire Cricket Club, supplied a most interesting document, the original contract signed between Copson and the club for the 1945 season. Tony Barker has kindly agreed reference to some of the material in his forthcoming book on the Bradford Cricket League. Philip Bailey has helped with the statistics of Copson's first-class career and his contemporaries. Eric Midwinter's eloquent foreword sets our subject in his social context. John Shawcroft, an expert on Derbyshire cricket, contributed advice on Copson's relationships with the county club and fellow players. Roger Mann and Patrick Jeater have contributed excellent photographs from their sources. David Frith helped with photograph identification. Four first-class cricketers – Tony Brown, Donald Carr, Mike Smith and Allan Watkins – have helped with their own recollections, given to Douglas Miller, of our subject as a player or umpire. David Jeater has edited the book and has brought to my attention much additional information about its subject from published and unpublished sources, points which have been gratefully incorporated into the narrative. My thanks too, to Zahra Ridge for her cover design and to Gerald Hudd and Chris Overson for their proofreading.

Bibliography

Regular publications and newspapers

Derbyshire County Cricket Club, *Yearbook* various years from 1954

Various Derbyshire and Yorkshire local newspapers, from 1927 onwards

News Chronicle Cricket Annual, from 1933 to 1951

The Cricketer magazine, from 1932 onwards

The Times, from 1932 onwards

Wisden Cricketers' Almanack, from 1933 onwards

Books

David Rayvern Allen, *Sir Aubrey* (Second Edition), J.W.McKenzie, 2005

Bill Andrews, *The Hand That Bowled Bradman,* Sportsmans Book Club, 1974

Gordon Andrews, *The Datasport Book of Wartime Cricket: 1940-45,* Datasport, 1990

David Baggett, *Derbyshire County Cricket Club: First Class Records 1871-1994,* Limlow Books, 1995

Antony Barker, *Cricket's Wartime Sanctuary,* unpublished

Nevill Cardus, *Australian Summer: The Test Matches of 1936-37,* Cape, 1937

Bill Frindall, *The Wisden Book of Cricket Records* (Fourth Edition), Headline, 1998

Edward Giles, *The Derbyshire Chronicles: Cricket's Lost and Found Championships 1874 and 1936,* Desert Island Books, 2007

S.C.Griffith, 'Sussex *v* Derbyshire', in John Arlott (ed.), *Cricket in the Counties,* Saturn Press, 1950

Walter Hammond, *Cricket My Destiny,* Stanley Paul, 1946

Bruce Harris, *1937 Test Tour,* Hutchinson, 1937

Jim Ledbetter (and Peter Wynne-Thomas), *First Class Cricket: A Complete Record,* various issues from 1932 to 1938, Limlow Books and 1939 Breedon Books, 1991 onwards

F.G.Peach and Philip Bailey, *Derbyshire Cricketers: 1871-1981,* Association of Cricket Statisticians, 1982

Peter Pickup, *History of the Bradford Cricket League 1903-1988*, Fairhaven Books, 1988

William Pollock, *So this is Australia*, Barker, 1937

Patsy Quinn, *Run of the Mill: A History of Saltaire Cricket Club*, Fire Horse Publications, 1997

Brian Rendell, *Gubby under Pressure*, ACS Publications, 2007

John Shawcroft, 'Bill Copson in the Border League', *The Cricket Statistician*, 122, 2003

John Shawcroft, *Local Heroes*, SportsBooks, 2006

John Shawcroft, *The History of Derbyshire County Cricket Club: 1870-1970*, Derbyshire County Cricket Club, 1970

John Shawcroft, *The History of Derbyshire County Cricket Club*, Christopher Helm, 1989

Ric Sissons, *The Players: A Social History of the Professional Cricketer*, The Kingswood Press, 1988

E.W.Swanton, *As I Said At The Time*, Willow Books, 1983

Philip Thorn, 'Just How Old Are You?', *The Cricket Statistician*, 112, 2000

David Thurlow, *Ken Farnes: The Diary of an Essex Master*, Parrs Wood Press, 2000

Pelham Warner, *Cricket Between Two Wars*, Chatto and Windus, 1942

Roy Webber, *County Cricket Championship: A History of the Competition from 1873*, Phoenix Sports Books, 1957

Roy Webber, *The Playfair Book of Cricket Records*, Playfair Books, 1951

Jack Williams, *Cricket and England*, Frank Cass, 1999

R.E.S.Wyatt, *Three Straight Sticks*, Stanley Paul and Co Ltd, 1951

Internet sources
In addition I have made good use of the websites at www.cricketarchive.com and www.bradfordcricketleague.org

Appendix
Some Statistics

Test cricket: Batting and Fielding

		M	I	NO	R	HS	Ave	100	50	Ct
1939	WI	2	-	-	-	-	-	-	-	1
1947	SA	1	1	0	6	6	6.00	-	-	-
Total		**3**	**1**	**0**	**6**	**6**	**6.00**	**-**	**-**	**1**

Test cricket: Bowling

		O	M	R	W	BB	Ave	5i	10m
1939	WI	52.4	7	185	12	5-85	15.41	1	-
1947	SA	57	24	112	3	3-46	37.33	-	-
Total	**(6b)**	**57**	**24⎫**	**297**	**15**	**5-85**	**19.80**	**1**	**-**
	(8b)	**52.4**	**7⎭**						

Note: There were eight balls in an over in 1939 and six in 1947.

First-Class cricket: Batting and Fielding

		M	I	NO	R	HS	Ave	100	50	Ct
1932	Eng	18	22	9	65	15	5.00	-	-	3
1933	Eng	26	33	7	172	43	6.61	-	-	9
1934	Eng	22	29	9	118	18	5.90	-	-	13
1935	Eng	18	23	9	134	22*	9.57	-	-	5
1936	Eng	31	34	15	135	24	7.10	-	-	17
1936/37	Aus/NZ	8	10	5	52	12	10.40	-	-	4
1937	Eng	17	22	10	135	30*	11.25	-	-	6
1938	Eng	24	29	8	68	12	3.23	-	-	8
1939	Eng	31	39	9	229	26	7.63	-	-	7
1946	Eng	25	35	11	99	18*	4.12	-	-	10
1947	Eng	21	31	6	210	38*	8.40	-	-	11
1948	Eng	10	9	1	82	19	10.25	-	-	7
1949	Eng	27	41	8	211	28	6.39	-	-	4
1950	Eng	1	2	1	1	1	1.00	-	-	-
Total		**279**	**359**	**108**	**1711**	**43**	**6.81**	**-**	**-**	**104**

Notes: Copson was dismissed 123 times bowled (49%); 95 times caught (38%); 17 times stumped (7%); ten times run out, and six times lbw. His highest score was 43, ct G.Duckworth b F.M.Sibbles, in Derbyshire's first innings against Lancashire at Stanley Park, Blackpool in 1933. He had five other scores of 25 or more. T.W.J.Goddard and P.F.Jackson both took his wicket eight times, more than any other bowlers.

First-Class cricket: Bowling

		O	M	R	W	BB	Ave	5i	10m
1932	Eng	568.5	142	1269	46	5-40	27.58	2	-
1933	Eng	818	226	1921	90	7-62	21.34	5	-
1934	Eng	697.2	169	1648	91	5-36	18.10	3	-
1935	Eng	500	113	1174	71	6-42	16.53	6	-
1936	Eng	946.4	239	2135	160	7-16	13.34	13	2
1936/37	Aus/NZ (6b)	33	8	535	27	4-32	19.81	-	-
	(8b)	131.7	15						
1937	Eng	495.1	101	1398	76	8-11	18.39	4	1
1938	Eng	742.4	156	1995	101	7-59	19.75	8	-
1939	Eng (8b)	668.3	93	2238	146	7-39	15.32	12	3
1946	Eng	803	191	1904	93	6-49	20.47	5	-
1947	Eng	766.4	202	1946	89	5-15	21.86	4	-
1948	Eng	246.3	58	590	31	7-103	19.03	1	-
1949	Eng	673.2	150	1902	71	5-23	26.78	3	-
1950	Eng	44	12	97	2	2-55	48.50	-	-
Total	**(6b)**	**7335.1**	**1767⎫**	**20752**	**1094**	**8-11**	**18.96**	**66**	**6**
	(8b)	**800.2**	**108⎭**						

Notes: There were eight balls in an over in Australia in 1936/37 and in England in 1939. In all other seasons there were six balls in an over, including New Zealand in 1936/37. Copson took wickets at the rate of one per 46.08 balls and conceded runs at a rate equivalent to 2.46 runs per six-ball over. Of his 1,094 wickets, 498 (46%) were bowled; 491 (45%) caught; 102 (9%) lbw; and three hit wicket. Of his 491 dismissals by catches, 173 were taken by identified wicket-keepers. He took the wicket of C.J.Barnett thirteen times, more than any other batsman who faced him.

First-Class cricket: Batting partnerships of fifty runs or more (3)

Runs	Partner	Match
80	A.W.Richardson	Derbyshire v Lancashire, Blackpool, 1933
70	G.O.B.Allen	MCC v Combined XI, Perth (W.A.), 1936/37
62	C.Gladwin	Derbyshire v Essex, Chesterfield, 1947

Note: All three partnerships were for the tenth wicket and in the side's first innings.

First-Class cricket: Five wickets or more in an innings (66)

Bowling	For	Opponent	Venue	Season
27-5-48-5	Derbyshire	Hampshire[1]	Southampton	1932
24-8-40-5	Derbyshire	Kent[2]	Tonbridge	1932
18.2-4-38-5	Derbyshire	Kent[1]	Derby	1933
23.1-8-59-5	Derbyshire	Sussex[1]	Eastbourne	1933
19-4-62-5	Derbyshire	Kent[1]	Canterbury	1933
28-6-62-7	Derbyshire	Gloucestershire[1]	Cheltenham College	1933
17.1-5-28-5	Derbyshire	Middlesex[1]	Lord's	1933
17.4-5-36-5	Derbyshire	Kent[1]	Tunbridge Wells	1934
20.3-5-63-5	Derbyshire	Middlesex[2]	Lord's	1934
19-5-40-5	Derbyshire	Nottinghamshire[2]	Ilkeston	1934
15-4-37-5	Derbyshire	Leicestershire[2]	Derby	1935
15-5-29-5	Derbyshire	Essex[1]	Brentwood	1935
8-3-15-5	Derbyshire	Somerset[2]	Derby	1935
19-8-31-5	Derbyshire	Gloucestershire[2]	Burton-on-Trent	1935

23.2-7-42-6	Derbyshire	Sussex[2]	Hove	1935
18-2-44-5	Derbyshire	Northamptonshire[2]	Northampton	1935
16-2-57-5	Derbyshire	Kent[1]	Gravesend	1936
16-6-33-5	Derbyshire	Surrey[1]	Derby	1936
14-5-19-7	Derbyshire	Surrey[2]	Derby	1936
17-5-42-5	Derbyshire	Sussex[1]	Chesterfield	1936
22-13-24-6	Derbyshire	Northamptonshire[2]	Northampton	1936
27-8-34-5	Derbyshire	Worcestershire[1]	Chesterfield	1936
18-2-38-5	Derbyshire	Worcestershire[1]	Worcester	1936
13-6-16-7	Derbyshire	Worcestershire[2]	Worcester	1936
25-9-44-5	Derbyshire	Indians[1]	Derby	1936
30-7-60-6	Derbyshire	Yorkshire[1]	Sheffield (Bramall Lane) 1936
18-5-40-5	Derbyshire	Leicestershire[1]	Derby	1936
35-8-87-6	Derbyshire	Sussex[1]	Eastbourne	1936
30-6-81-6	Derbyshire	Somerset[2]	Wells	1936
21.4-2-73-5	Derbyshire	Lancashire[1]	Burton-on-Trent	1937
8.2-2-11-8	Derbyshire	Warwickshire[1]	Derby	1937
23-0-99-5	Derbyshire	Essex[1]	Ilkeston	1937
17.5-2-64-8	Derbyshire	Sussex[1]	Derby	1937
28-9-54-5	Derbyshire	Lancashire[1]	Liverpool	1938
24.3-7-51-5	Derbyshire	Warwickshire[1]	Derby	1938
16-5-26-5	Derbyshire	Northamptonshire[1]	Northampton	1938
27-2-75-5	Derbyshire	Gloucestershire[1]	Burton-on-Trent	1938
24.5-9-59-7	Derbyshire	Nottinghamshire[2]	Ilkeston	1938
21-4-36-6	Derbyshire	Warwickshire[2]	Edgbaston	1938
16.2-6-38-6	Derbyshire	Worcestershire[2]	Derby	1938
19-1-65-5	Derbyshire	Nottinghamshire[1]	Trent Bridge	1938
6-2-12-5	Derbyshire	Oxford University[1]	The Parks	1939
4.7-2-9-5	Derbyshire	Oxford University[2]	The Parks	1939
17-4-47-5	Derbyshire	Surrey[1]	Chesterfield	1939
14-2-47-5	Derbyshire	Warwickshire[1]	Edgbaston	1939
13-2-39-5	Derbyshire	Kent[1]	Ilkeston	1939
19.4.1-73-6	Derbyshire	West Indians[1]	Derby	1939
24-4-85-5	England	West Indies[1]	Lord's	1939
20.4-4-64-6	Derbyshire	Sussex[1]	Derby	1939
17.1-3-57-6	Derbyshire	Essex[1]	Chesterfield	1939
11-2-39-7	Derbyshire	Middlesex[2]	Derby	1939
13-1-45-5	Derbyshire	Gloucestershire[1]	Cheltenham	1939
14.6-3-39-6	Derbyshire	Leicestershire[1]	Leicester (Aylestone Rd) 1939
23.3-10-26-5	Derbyshire	Kent[1]	Chesterfield	1946
20-6-49-6	Derbyshire	Sussex[2]	Sheffield (Abbeydale Pk) 1946
20-9-29-5	Derbyshire	Glamorgan[2]	Chesterfield	1946
25-4-68-5	Derbyshire	Northamptonshire[1]	Derby	1946
15.4-5-37-5	Derbyshire	Somerset[1]	Frome	1946
14-3-39-5	Derbyshire	Warwickshire[1]	Edgbaston	1947
17.1-4-21-5	Derbyshire	Leicestershire[2]	Ilkeston	1947
20.1-10-25-5	Derbyshire	Lancashire[2]	Buxton	1947
14-5-15-5	Derbyshire	Worcestershire[1]	Worcester	1947
38.3-6-103-7	Derbyshire	Warwickshire[1]	Derby	1948
20-8-43-5	Derbyshire	Essex[2]	Westcliff-on-Sea	1949
16-6-34-5	Derbyshire	Somerset[1]	Taunton	1949
14.5-7-23-5	Derbyshire	Essex[1]	Burton-on-Trent	1949

Notes: There were eight balls in an over in England in 1939. The returns listed above include Copson's three hat tricks in first-class cricket. These were all for Derbyshire, two in 1937 v Lancashire at Burton-on-Trent and v Warwickshire at Derby, the latter of which became four wickets in four balls; and one in 1939 v Oxford University at The Parks.

First-Class cricket: Ten wickets or more in a match (6)

Bowling	For	Opponent	Venue	Season
12-52 (5-33 and 7-19)				
	Derbyshire	Surrey	Derby	1936
12-54 (5-38 and 7-16)				
	Derbyshire	Worcestershire	Worcester	1936
11-93 (8-11 and 3-82)				
	Derbyshire	Warwickshire	Derby	1937
10-21 (5-12 and 5-9)				
	Derbyshire	Oxford University	The Parks	1939
10-78 (6-57 and 4-21)				
	Derbyshire	Essex	Chesterfield	1939
10-92 (6-73 and 4-19)				
	Derbyshire	West Indians	Derby	1939

Sources for all seven tables: First-Class Cricket: A Complete Record, various years; and www.cricketarchive.com